Sensitive
Permaculture
Cultivating the way of the sacred Earth

Alanna Moore

Python Press

Alanna Moore is the author of:
Backyard Poultry – Naturally' 1998
Stone Age Farming 2001
Divining Earth Spirit 1994, 2004 (2nd ed.)
The Magic of Menhirs & Circles of Stone 2005
The Wisdom of Water 2007
Water Spirits of the World 2008

Sensitive Permaculture
ISBN – 978-0-9757782-2-7
is published by Python Press
www.pythonpress.com
pythonpress@gmail.com
PO Box 929
Castlemaine Vic 3450
Australia

Text, design, photographs and most illustrations
by Alanna Moore (except where noted)

Printed by Lightning Source

Dedicated with much love and thanks to my husband Peter Cowman
and to the teachers, friends and colleagues who have given assistance
and shared the way.

Front cover: Permaculture herb spiral garden, Frog Pond,
            Power Tower and boggy meadows of Síog in Ireland.

Introduction

Like a lush and unruly garden itself, *Sensitive Permaculture* is a celebration of the sanctity of Mother Earth, indigenous Earth lore and the continuing traditions of nature based spirituality.

For the past 26 years I have worked as a geomancer, assessing and balancing the subtle energies of places; while for the past 22 years I have also been a keen permaculture practitioner. Permaculture is the ethical design of sustainable culture. Implementing a geomantic permaculture design for sustainable food production and living helps to alleviate environmental problems on many levels. Nowadays I'm finding that such a sensitive approach to land planning and Earth care is gaining a welcome resonance amongst people who are weary of the negativity and unsustainability of today's society.

For me, nature reverence includes the invisible dimensions of landscape. I divide my time between Australia and Ireland, both places where knowledge of geomancy and the fairy world has survived relatively well, in understated undercurrents at the least. The Australian Aborigines and native Irish are highly intuitive peoples. Like other animist societies, the Irish believed that fairy beings help to care for their crops and livestock, thus the 'Good People' must always be thanked, and their homes and pathways respected.

Nature spirits continue to be a dynamic force in the landscape, I've discovered in my life of professional dowsing experience, travel and teaching. By pendulum dowsing and meditative attunement I can find exactly where these beings are stationed and thus avoid disturbing them. In this book I explain how eliciting nature's help in the garden can foster harmonious feng shui, as well as nourish our own inner, spiritual gardens.

Sensitive Permaculture focuses on an energetic, loving approach to sustainable land planning, for when we connect to the sacred dimensions of life our activities become positively life-affirming and joyful.

My great hope is that this book helps to make a contribution to sustaining the sacred life of precious planet Earth.

Contents

Reverence of nature celebrated in an
Indian sculpture, British Museum.

Chapter 1: Sacred Perspectives

The sacred landscape

In traditional paradigms of indigenous peoples the world over, all living beings have intrinsic sacred value. The land itself embodies sacredness and some places, in particular, are more sacred than others. Theirs is an Earth based spirituality and thus they dwell in the divine.

Since earliest times people have visited the networks of sacred sites to connect deeply with the Earth spirit, ancestors, deities and beings of the land. Sacred Aboriginal Increase sites in Australia, for instance, are where people go to communicate with the spirits of animals they hunt and plants they gather, in order to encourage their fruitfulness. Totemic laws of Aboriginal society provide a degree of protection for particular plants and animals, due to people's spiritual bonds with them.

The eco-spiritual approach to Earth care, as the Aboriginals have inherited, fosters the symbiosis of all beings to live in balance in a holy, wholesome eco-system. Such a scenario might be imagined to have also endured over past millennia as the Golden Ages of other cultures. These eras no doubt lasted until people outgrew a region, ushering in tribal wars for territory and resources, and cultural collapse.

It wasn't too long ago, however, that rural Europeans lived in far greater harmony with their environment. The peasant populace enjoyed a great love of the lands that sustained them, treasured their fields and live-stock, and protected their trees. Lives of simplicity were joyful, with simple pleasures abundant. Nobody needed psychoanalysis, the social networks were caring and strong. Work was often hard, but there were always sacred times to rest and be re-created, to make pilgrimage to the local sacred spring or mountain, and enjoy the fun of community festivities in the yearly cycle of agrarian activities.

In many parts of the world this type of scenario is still the case. Westerners who visit such less-wealthy countries are struck by the high level of human joyfulness, the radiant smiles, the kindness and hospitality of people who have nothing much in terms of possessions, but who are rich in spirit. It reveals to us clearly that 'less is more'.

Diminuation of 'resources'

In today's over-industrialised world land and nature are degradingly classed as 'resources', as things to be plundered wholesale. The Western lifestyle is taking more than its fair share of Gaia's gifts and also undervalues them enormously. It's like the parable of killing the goose that lays the golden eggs - an ancient plea for the conservation of nature's treasures.

When we tear off too much of the fabric of life we can upset the balance big-time. An extinction of just one species from a society of beings can lead to a domino effect of eco-system collapse. Nature is not the only one suffering as a result. Already, bee colony collapse is pandemic and it can lead to widespread crop loss and famine from a lack of pollination.

We are barely aware of the complexity of relationships between species, while the reductionist path of Science ignores the wholeness of life. Nature is a mysterious mistress and we gain enormously by listening to Her and also to our own wilder, intuitive self. (Most people can easily hone their intuitive skills by learning the art of pendulum dowsing, I've found.)

In today's warped society we can't trust Science to save us from environmental ills, not when it is underwritten by vested interests that manipulate research and push toxic products. Science has been said to be purely all 'fame and funding' these days. If past pronouncements have been made that 'Pan is dead', and, later, that 'God is dead', perhaps we must now proclaim that Science is mostly dead now, too?

Living traditions

Visiting Buddhist countries in Asia I am always struck by the relatively gentle atmosphere pervading society. Buddhists recognise that all of nature is sentient and exudes intelligence, in varying degrees. Thus they are careful to treat all beings accordingly, with kindness and compassion. They honour the spirits of the land and sky, reverently tending the household spirit shrines on a daily basis. Around such places I can feel those loving intentions permeating the atmosphere.

Coming, as Westerners do, from more of a spiritual vacuum, many are now trying to re-capture the sacred by turning to Buddhism and other exotic spiritual paths. The personal benefits, from meditation and empowering psychological paradigms, are undeniable. But what kindness do they display in relation to their environment? Are pagans the experts when it comes to Earth harmony?

Pagans claim to maintain age-old, pre-Christian traditions indigenous to various parts of Europe, Siberia or elsewhere. But in reality these are generally neo-pagan traditions and they do not necessarily rate as eco-spiritual.

Most people who profess to be pagans and who live in cities are probably content with dressing up (or down!) for rituals and more of the social aspects, which can be fun and harmless. But pagan networks also facilitate fabulous Earth care activities, such as pagan environmental activist groups.

It's interesting how the fringe activities of the pagans are becoming mainstream these days. Twenty five years ago people in a village in Victoria would tell their children to keep away from my friends, who were the organisers of an annual pagan festival there. But nowadays the whole school gets involved with some of their seasonal festivals. I attended a wonderful winter solstice event one year, where all the kids were circle dancing!

Perhaps this evolving change in thinking was spurred on when scientist James Lovelock described Earth as a living being, which he respectfully dubbed Gaia, after the old Greek goddess. His concept, taken seriously, leads to a weight of responsibility and if we want our planet to survive, the recognition of a living Gaia is a good starting point. The Sacred Way of Gaia involves planting trees, saving seeds, dealing with our waste and making compost too.

Animism

I call myself an animist. It is a term that carries much less baggage than pagan, which originally meant 'people of the land'. As an animist I recognise that spirits are everywhere, they are an aspect of all living things and they're also found in rocks and the elements too. Some spirits have been empowered by human reverence and deified over the course of human history. These have become the many gods and goddesses, and there are also fairy 'kings' and 'queens'. Often these highly evolved beings help humankind with their magical, oracular or healing powers. They certainly don't intend any harm to us, as some people's church-derived fears might expect, unless we have caused them grief.

I like to communicate with the spirits of nature and honour them. They show me things and enlighten me. I acknowledge the wisdom of nature and try to give back to Gaia as much as She gives me. Or more. As a geomancer, I know there is much work to be done to discover Her wounds and heal the gaping scars in the land. I am training up many more to tackle these problems.

The Western industrial mindset can be mind-numbingly powerful. A grassroots return to sacred values can help loosen its stifling grip and provide our lives with a greater sense of meaning as well. Solutions to our loss of harmony with nature lie not only in philosophies gleaned from far-off lands, but also from the indigenous traditions of the land, the inherent Earth wisdom that's all around us and which can be directly divined.

We don't need to go far to find the Holy Land. It is under our feet. If we learn how to listen to the sacred land and work co-creatively with Her, greater Earth harmony can be achieved. And simple solutions to global environmental problems can begin in our very own backyards.

Chapter 2: What is permaculture?

Final frontiers

On a voyage of discovery sailing the lonely south-west Pacific Ocean, after days of searching you finally catch sight of a sliver of land on the blue horizon. A small island of volcanic origin is thrusting upwards out of the vast expanse of blue. It's Tikopia, a tiny nation that has been inhabited for over two millennia.

As you get closer, you marvel at the dense tropical jungle blanketing the island. But later you learn that not much of this is actual wild jungle at all. Rather, it is all highly managed food forests of edible and useful tree, shrub, vine and groundcover species, integrated together in a wonderful example of companion planting. These jungle orchards have been the mainstay of the Tikopian peoples' diet, which only needs supplementation with fish from the surrounding reef. Everyone there has enough to eat and sustain a satisfying life.

In Jared Diamond's 'Collapse', Tikopia is cast as an epitome of sustainable culture. The population has stabilised to around 700, which the islanders have identified as being best for long term survival. In past times the population became dangerously high and when the usually reliable rains didn't come and crops failed, causing widespread starvation, people were forced to take off in canoes to the open sea, a form of suicide. There were no more suitable vacant islands left to go to.

At times in Tikopia's history the island's four tribal groups would regularly wage war upon each other and murder was rife. Eventually everyone agreed to stop warring and to also stop keeping pigs, because they required too much food - food that people could be eating. Nowadays tribal chiefs preside over community meetings where the main topic is family planning. Peace reigns and Tikopia presents a rare example of people striking a dynamic, sacred balance with their environment, whereby all parties are enabled to achieve a simple, but enjoyable quality of life.

Tikopia is a tiny version of planet Earth. We have pretty much filled Her up with humans and there's nowhere else for us to go. The time has come to learn to live within our planetary means and place limits on growth, if our descendents are to survive in peace and contentment. For food security we need to revive our gardener genes and grow food wherever we can and without relying on fossil fuels.

Tikopia is blessed by fertile volcanic soils and regular rainfall to (usually) guarantee good harvests. Elsewhere on the planet most other lands are not so hospitable and life isn't so easy. True sustainability will require many creative solutions. Fundamental changes are needed to achieve what a tiny island in the remote Pacific achieved centuries ago. Conversely, current Western approaches to sustainability seem more to do with maintaining the status quo.

For a truly sustainable future it's not hard to figure out that Gaia urgently needs positive energy and will power, some seed funding and a smart, systematic approach to land planning. Fortunately such a system already exists. It's called permaculture.

Permaculture design

The word permaculture is a combination of permanent and culture (also permanent agriculture). It aims for the long term sustainability of food production and human settlements. Bill Mollison and David Holmgren developed the permaculture design system in Australia over 30 years ago and it has gone on to be highly successful at increasing the food security of communities across the world.

Permaculture design provides home grown, backyard solutions to global environmental problems. Permaculture food gardens and farms are characterised by small scale, intensive land-use patterns where one works as close as possible to home. A high diversity of yields is obtained from a wide variety of species, ranging from wild foods and seedlings to domesticated cultivars, and with an emphasis on perennial plants, all growing in a range of niches and microclimates.

Permaculture looks to nature as the supreme guide for modelling sustainability. The inherent stability of natural forests and the complex web of relationships within them provide a premier model of co-operation and inter-dependence between plants and animals. Food forest gardens, so symbolic of good permaculture design, epitomise this eco-systems approach to edible landscape planning.

The natural systems that permaculture gardens emulate are characterised by endless cycles of decay and renewal, and these maintain the bio-chemical cycles of essential elements. Humans need around 30 essential minerals and elements for optimum survival, but chemically farmed foods rarely provide us with them, while their production impacts heavily on the environment with high carbon, nitrogen and phosphorus footprints. Permaculture farmers are encouraged to replace minerals lost from the soil as a result of food production. (This can be well achieved with the addition of crushed basalt stone and home-made compost.)

In permaculture design the naturally inherent traits of the land and its flora and fauna are discovered and utilised, with minimal external inputs brought in. One works with and harnesses the natural energies and elements, such as sun, wind, rain, gravity and soil, in order to obtain a yield. The range of energies investigated can also include the subtle energies found by geobiologists and geomancers, such as I dowse for in a professional capacity.

Permaculture thought urges us to use the gifts of the Earth to their highest capacity (not putting purified drinking water down the toilet, for instance). Elements to be incorporated into one's landscape design are selected for multi-functionality and one always plans to work where it counts, in order to make things pay. No room for unproductive lawns and concrete in the yard! There's food to be grown, and as close as possible to where it's going to be eaten!

One's personal energy is conserved by using a system of zoning that, when illustrated, looks like ripples in a pond that radiate outwards from the home. Permaculture zoning determines the placement of high to low

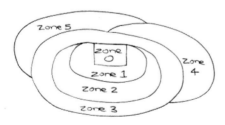

maintenance plants and animals requiring our care. Briefly speaking, Zone Zero is our home and inner world, Zone One has high maintenance food production close to home; Zone Two is for the intensive orchard and small livestock; further out Zone Three might be main crops, seedling orchard or pasture with larger livestock; Zone

Four can be a forestry area beyond that; while a Zone Five wilderness area is generally on the outer fringe of the property and rarely visited.

Self-reliance as well as community inter-dependence is the permaculture way. Growing food in excess, one shares the surplus, as well as sharing ideas, money and energy, which are best kept constantly circulating around one's local community.

With its ethics based approach, permaculture provides the perfect buffer to global environmental and financial instability. Caring for people and the planet is the permaculture catchcry.

Eco-spiritual approach

I feel it's time for permaculturalists to seek another, more sensitive level of relationship with landscape. An eco-spiritual, indigenous approach to custodianship of the land can deepen our connection with nature and love of Country. It can propel us from our hearts and give us courage to passionately protect our environment.

Permaculturists have been accused of imposing alien ideas, weed plants and species that may not be suited. For example an Italian designer who was brought in to consult for an Irish eco-village advocated swathes of olive trees, where certainly none of these would have a chance of survival. Some permaculture teachers show great cultural insensitivities to students in cultures outside of their own. This has even happened in Ireland, where fairy lore has come under attack.

A sensitive approach helps us to design edible landscapes for indigenous people in different lands, paying due respect to ancient animistic beliefs, rather than acting out the 'well-meaning' stance of past colonial tyrants. With an unburdening of any colonial mentality, we can incorporate a more sensitive assessment of place and plan appropriately, following age-old traditions. We can forge a dynamic connection to the land by listening to what it has to say to us, in a joyful spirit of co-operation. And ideally this process is begun long before any major land-use decisions are made.

Chapter 3: Slow Living

Slow cooking

Our Solar Box Cooker is made from cardboard boxes that were gleaned from outside an electrical goods store. These were cut down and glued together by Peter into an open box measuring 1m by 70cm by 70cm. A second box a bit smaller was then made to sit on little feet inside the larger one. The outside was finished off with paper sheets fixed with wallpaper paste, with aluminium foil pasted inside as a reflective liner.

Between the inner and outer boxes of the cooker we stuffed home-grown llama fleece for snug insulation. Finally an old window was placed on top for the sun to shine through and heat up the insulated space. After a couple of weeks of fiddling around and scrounging for useful waste materials, Peter had created our first solar hot box and with great excitement we were thrilled to start to cook with it.

And so we brought dishes to the boil, then transferred them over to the box to slowly cook over the several hours. Success! Tasty rice and beans! Yummy soups! Even scones worked well in Peter's delicious experiments. We noted possible refinements of adding an opening box lid that could act as a reflector to increase solar radiation in the box. But why bother? This was the ultimate in slow food and could we ever taste the difference! And no need to check the cooking food meant we were freed up on time spent in the kitchen. We just needed to plan well ahead, such as by soaking beans the night before we wanted them for the following evening's meal.

Everything cooked in that box tasted so wonderful! Beans - simply the best! And could the sun perhaps be imparting the food with special qualities, such that are absent in fast cooked foods? Certainly, food that has been stored in a refrigerator and then rapidly cooked with either electrical or microwave energies never tastes this good and is potentially more unhealthy to consume. As well, I've found that the ch'i of such degraded food, it's energy bio-field, has in the process been greatly reduced, meaning less nutritional goodness for us, and allowing it to putrefy more rapidly. I can measure such energetic bio-effects with my dowsing pendulum.

Solar cooking would have to be the most planet friendly way to get a feed, although if you are in short supply of hot sunny days, then a Haybox Cooker can be a good alternative. This is a highly insulated box (or basket) which takes a cooking pot that has been brought to the boil, retaining all of its heat for slow cooking over several hours. Often a feather pillow or two is stuffed around the top of the cook pot and an insulated lid placed over that, to reduce heat leakage.

Slow down

So it saves energy and money and tastes better. Those are just some of the benefits of the Way of Slowness, or Slow Living, an idea that embraces much more than just food. The Slow Food movement has set the scene for slowing things down on a much grander scale.

Already the global economy has taken up the cause of Slowing Down, but I'm anxiously awaiting the world's startled leaders to have a reality check and relax into the challenge of it. Like athletes on steroids, society has been on the raceway to disaster, hyperventilating with unprecedented rates of rapid growth in dirty industries like mining, food and power production, and spewing hideous pollution of all kinds in all directions. It couldn't go on. The race had to stop.

To maintain the out of control hyper world we have been forced to work very fast (or lose our job!), so that we can drive fast cars, get fast loans and fast food. Not surprisingly, the level of hyperactivity in society and lack of down-time is sickening! Stress related disorders are rampant.

Television film editors bombard us with nano-second long images and sound bites which appear to presume a high level of Attention Deficit Disorder in the population. Or perhaps they are the afflicted ones. We are expected to be slaves of mobile phone technology so as to be totally available and trackable, while being barraged with experimental doses of dangerous radiation frequencies. What kind of life is this? And we exchange our time at work for it? Surely we are the biggest losers in the transaction.

Rather than following the consumer lemming crowd all racing towards the unknown and squabbling together, society has only one option.
Slow down. Take a few breaths. Take stock. Go green.

Living slow

These days people seem to have forgotten all sorts of skills in the kitchen. They buy ready made food dips, yoghurts and sprouted seeds, not thinking about how long these might have been languishing on the shop shelf, or what preservatives have been added. In my youth I delighted in making fresh pestos and yoghurt, and grew sprouts in jars on window ledges. (You couldn't buy such things then anyway.) I even discovered that yoghurt could make itself! On a hot day a forgotten jar of fresh milk straight from the goat turned itself into yoghurt.

I've never been one for electrical kitchen appliances either. Slowly you get there in the end. Making delicious meals can take some time but it gives me time to think, watch the birds out the window and just enjoy the experience of cooking. And besides, all that electricity and metal tends to taint the food quality.

When I water the garden I also prefer the slow approach. I could have laid miles of pipes to drip irrigate my plants, which itself is a soundly slow method, but I prefer to select plants that can thrive in the extremes of a highly variable climate (in Victoria) without extra watering, apart from establishing them by hand watering with a can. This is said to be the most efficient form of water delivery and I can only agree. Hand watering can provide an enjoyable spot of exercise while nothing gets blasted by the hose. Seedlings, in particular, don't really appreciate being water blasted to bits! Collecting rain water from the roof for this purpose, I also add my own fresh urine (at 20%) to fertilise plants at the same time. The plants love it!

For a treat, I love the Slow Indulgence of a Fire Bath to slowly relax in and be deeply cleansed in the Great Outdoors of the garden. The old cast iron bathtub sits on the ground over the top of a small fire pit. Heating the water is a slow process that I allocate 2 – 3 hours for. If it's done with too big a fire and faster, the iron bath gets too hot to handle.

Steeping myself in it in a sort of sacred soup, I prefer the softness of rainwater and if I have to use tap water, at least the slow heating drives off chlorine. Bunches of aromatics herbs, such as Eau de Cologne and Chocolate Mint, are lovely to infuse in water as it heats, imparting saponins for lathering up and perfumed oils. Seaweeds are great too.

My top-of-the-range fire bath in Australia.

Lounging in such an aromatic hot tub, sitting on a bit of wood to stop the bum burning, is pure luxury. A glorious hour or more is well spent lying in the Great Outdoors, watching the sunset and then micro-bats flitting around beneath twinkling stars. No more tired muscles or problems of getting to sleep afterwards! Skin can become super soft too, if I put a handful of rolled oats into an old sock, soak it in the bathwater then wash with the squeezed out oat milk. If the body is truly our temple - this is a great way to soak into the Divine! Luckily for us, Heaven really is on Earth.

To live slowly one needs to free up on time. I choose to have a lifestyle where there is always time enough to read, watch the clouds float by, treat my body to yoga stretches and my mind to meditation and many interests. Having gone for a low stress lifestyle, such activities are usually enough to keep me totally happy and healthy.

Still mind

Meditation is the ultimate in energy saving. The do-nothing time is totally eco-friendly! Slowing down the mind with meditation also has numerous, well attested physical health and psychological benefits. Calmness is cultivated and becomes natural and pervasive.

Meditation is an entrainment technique that slows down the activity of our brainwaves. When we are in busy everyday thought mode we have a high level of beta waves generated in our brains. These are the fast ones, at up to around 30 cycles per second (Hertz). When we are in a high beta state it's difficult to be receptive. That requires a slower state of mind.

When we begin to meditate we slow down and go into an altered state of consciousness, where beta waves are reduced and the slower alpha waves start to predominate. In deeper meditation a steady alpha state can develop and even slower theta waves will begin to develop as well. In theta we can tap into deep levels of self-healing, problem solving and creativity inherent in us. In a steady alpha/theta state we can achieve a heightened state of receptivity and sensitivity. If we cultivate these states by regular meditation it becomes a much easier matter to better sense the subtle ch'i of things, feel each other's moods and the moods of places too.

Slow get around

When it comes to getting around there's nothing better than slowing down to a bicycle or walking pace for pure enjoyment of the environment. Being enclosed in a vehicle travelling fast, on the other hand, can easily disconnect us from nature. If we do need to get somewhere fast, let it be by train or bus and leave the bicycle at the station, for a more relaxing trip. I love to look at landscapes through train windows and I get the feeling that the environment sends me love back!

On slow journeys, by allocating plenty of time to get from A to B, who knows what adventures might ensue? And as you experience your locale slowly and directly, the sun on your cheek and wind on your face, you develop familiarity and intimacy with it. You feel the changing seasons in your body and explore the changes these bring. You get to know

Country and start to feel your way into its subtle levels of being. And thus you prepare yourself to discover the deeper, Dreaming layers of the land, of which we will soon be focussing.

There are sacred forms of walking too. Making pilgrimages on foot to sacred centres has long been popular and spiritually rewarding. Japanese people go to forests for 'Wood Air Bathing', absorbing the aromas and essences of the forest by walking and relaxing in them.

In a global megalithic revival, people are nowdays constructing stone circles wherein they conduct rituals and go for walking meditations, slowly perambulating around and around inside the circle in a meditative state.

The labyrinth is another classic form used for walking meditation. Some people are truly transformed by a labyrinth experience, with psychological knots unravelling on their walking journeys, which are mini-pilgrimages in themselves.

From walking the small white quartz labyrinth at 'Mucklestone' in central Victoria, my feeling is that the brain hemispheres become better balanced from doing this. Peter and I incorporated a labyrinth walk into our wedding ceremony, which was held outdoors there. Having drawn a nut from a bag to find out who would go first, I lead Peter into the centre of the labyrinth, where we exchanged our vows. Then he lead the way back out and we made our marriage declarations. It felt very special indeed.

Going slowly and discovering the sacredness of all life seem, to me, to go very much hand in hand. But how to get out of the fast lane?

Peter and Alanna's wedding ceremony
at the labyrinth at Mucklestone, 17/4/08.
Photo - Eliza Tree.

Chapter 4: Sustainability and Dreaming

Sustaining our dreams

Everyone wants to get rich, don't they? Voices in the new-age movement proclaim that abundance is our birthright, wealth a sign of self-worth. This seems not much different to society urging us to acquire all the things we've ever wanted, thus pumping up economic growth. Selling books that validate dreams of riches are a very good seller themselves, methinks! Certainly the film and book 'The Secret' have done well in promoting the cult of desire fulfilment.

"Visualise you are driving that big car you always wanted" says somebody in The (so-called) Secret. Trouble is, such aspirations don't mesh very well with the reality of today's world. Not everyone in the world can have the over-sized car, house or toys, plus a giant environmental impact in the process, can they now?

No doubt our genetic coding, shaped by memories of lean times or famine, harbours a certain degree of inherent greed. But by producing food close to home we can satisfy underlying food insecurity issues and yes, it is good to be thinking positively about yourself and life, I'm a great believer and exponent of that. But without limiting consumption, we risk planetary survival. The Secret of getting what we want is that there is No Secret. 'Work hard and you'll get lucky' they say. What we do need, however, is to manifest a higher plan!

Still we can also nurture our innermost dreams of what we would like to be doing with our lives to reach satisfaction on a soul level, for true health, wealth and fulfilment. Our dreams need realism and connection to the dreams of Gaia. And we need a way of moderating our desires that won't bankrupt our lives with debt.

How can this be achieved? I think there is a need to cultivate the Art of Contentment with life. To accept what life gives us and just enjoy it as it is, without having to fuss about changing everything to better suit us. Why bother with extreme renovations of a new home when you can be more patient and wait to find a place that better suits your needs? You might have a geriatric television or an older model car. As long as they do the job and work perfectly well, why upgrade?

Accepting life as it is, with gratitude in our hearts, can be a key to living happily within one's means. Resisting the evils of advertising is a lot easier when one practises the Art of Contentment. You won't need the latest fashion or status symbol when you are deeply contented, feeling good, your inner beauty shining radiantly.

Yes, abundance can be yours as well! Abundant good times with your friends and family, when you have enough time to spend with them. Abundant goodwill, abundant love. These things cannot be bought for money.

In some cultures it is the capacity to give that is the most valued trait in a person. People of wealth are distinguished only by how much they give away. Perhaps we should also aspire to abundant giving as a source of joy and satisfaction.

There is so much to learn from such ancient wisdom, once thought of as 'primitive'. Seems to me the over-industrialised nations are the primitive ones, with their lack of environmental awareness and Earth care.

Sustaining Earth's Dreaming

Not usually recognised in Western societies is that the Earth also has it's own inherent wisdom. The Dreaming or Dreamtime is the name of the spiritual reality of nature which informs and inspires Australian Aboriginal paradigms. (The English words being only a very approximate translation of the concept.) This understanding is found in many other parts of the world as well. Tibetans also recognise the presence of wisdom in nature, with 'mind treasures' received as divine inspiration, available to sensitive souls from birds, trees, light and space.

The Earth's Dreaming has memory too. To use Theosophical terminology, the 'Akashic Records' contain historical events that are recorded into the energetic fabric of a place. Partly historical, the Dreaming of the Earth is really an other-dimensional continuum, wherein Aboriginal totemic identification revolves around associations and responsibilities connected to the Dreaming of particular places.

As a geomancer I love to delve into the Dreaming dimensions of the land, which, in Australia, can be particularly profound. Where landscapes are not completely altered, the Dreaming is the dynamic character of a place, forged from its eco-spiritual, energetic, topographic, geological and historic dimensions. Dowsing, or divining, can be employed as a means of discovering the subtle Dreaming nature of places, as is meditation at key points in the landscape. Both approaches can help us to forge a deep connection to the environment.

In the Dreaming continuum all life is sentient and potentially available for us to interact with. Tribal Aboriginal people go through several levels of initiation over the course of their life whereby secrets of the Dreaming are gradually revealed to them, with simple mythos taking on ever deeper meanings over time. The mythic stories tend to reveal deep ethics of environmental care. (To learn more of the Aboriginal way of conveying wisdom I highly recommend the book 'Treading Lightly')

Buddhism also supports the animist view of nature consciousness, as do indigenous paradigms worldwide, from Shinto traditions of Japan to the fairy lore of Ireland. Entities who inhabit the Dreaming are not of our dimension, rather they are spirit beings of the devic kingdoms, 'devas' being a catch-all term from India that I shall refer to them by.

Of all cultures globally, it is the Aboriginal deep connection to Dreaming that has remained intact over the longest time span. Aboriginals express a passionate reverence that is audible whenever they speak of 'Country', that is, land belonging to their kin group for thousands of years and intimately known by them. Elsewhere, unfortunately, such paradigms have been largely suppressed by colonialism and missionaries over the past two millennia . However, despite this, the once pan-global world-view is still faintly etched onto peoples' psyches and genes. It can sometimes be pieced together from a survey of fragmentary legends or place-names and confirmed by visiting sites for direct experiential studies.

This I have been doing in Ireland, finding that you only have to scratch a thin veneer to find ancient pagan practices being upheld in the guise of Catholicism. The Dreaming of Ireland has been maintained in many places with traditions of pilgrimage to honour sacred sites, such as walking en-masse to the summit of holy mountain Croagh Patrick on the last Sunday in July, at the traditional start of harvest. This is no doubt a legacy of sacred agriculture rites originating from back in earliest times.

As the Dreamtime is a concept conveying the timeless other-worldy, other-dimensional qualities of place, I think it's a useful term to help us recapture those ancient understandings, anywhere and everywhere. Gaia the Earth spirit is alive and She is yearning for us to tap into Her very soul!

To research the Dreaming, one may find traditions remembered in original place names and local mythos that has been kept alive by elders or village story tellers (the Irish seanchaí, pronounced shanachy, for example). But the physical heritage may well be lost. It's all too easy for a bulldozer to quickly erase once sacred landforms or ancient monuments that may have taken decades or centuries to construct in the distant past. Although physically obliterated, however, the old memories of a site may persist and new ones of rape and pillage by earth-moving equipment are then deposited. The stories of place build up in layers, together with any associated intense trauma or emotion that then taints the local ch'i.

When we damage the Earth we are also damaging ourselves and Earth memories may haunt us, influencing our lives detrimentally. Humans are a terribly destructive lot, but we are also capable of creating outstanding beauty and harmony in the world. We just need to choose the latter, give ourselves a spiritual 'fright-break' and get on with making a better world.

What is the Dreaming of your local area? Perhaps an elderly neighbour knows something of it, or of someone else who does? As you walk around your district and tune into it sensitively you may well garner something of its subtle qualities. When you get to know it, you need to respect it for what it is and find out if its energies are meshing harmoniously with your own life.

Discover your local sacred sites and protect them from inappropriate developments in whatever way you can. Sacred sites often have few friends to care for them these days. Adopting a favourite sacred site you might visit it regularly, clearing away rubbish and leaving only your love.

By such activities we Renew the Dreaming of places in subtle ways and we find greater meaning for ourselves in terms of feeling at home in an area and living in harmony with the sacred.

Chapter 5: Earth awareness, self awareness

Early peoples of the Old World, and many tribal people still today, exercised great sensitivity and awareness of the environment to which they felt intimately related. The Earth's electro-magnetic field strength was around 50% stronger in Neolithic times, so no doubt the energies and devas of the land were more easily perceivable then.

Human awareness of the environment has been on a downward spiral pretty much ever since those times. Early monotheistic religion put man on a pedestal and in particular the men who followed the favoured god. This fuelled gross abuses, such as the excuse to wage genocidal invasions of other peoples' lands and cultures. Earth Dreamings have suffered terribly as a consequence.

Today we have to try a bit harder to develop our inherent sensitivity, which our standard education system generally ignores. At school (apart from Steiner education) we are only encouraged to develop logical thought processes, as if we only needed to use half our brain. Learning to dowse, we can redress the imbalance and develop more balanced ways of thinking. We can even re-learn to think with our hearts.

Colonisation

Two lands, far distant, but their inhabitants connected genetically to each other. Each once packed with ancient treasures of indigenous wisdom, sacred and magical places and the legacies of powerful heroes, gods and goddesses, and deified ancestors. Each suffering similar histories of the shameful maltreatment of its native peoples and degradation of lands by British colonial forces. I write about Ireland and Australia, where I divide my time. When I travel between the two countries my realisation of the consequences of all this history is piqued.

Insidious effects of colonisation are still warping many people's psyches today, it seems to me. Colonisers often forcibly indocrinated victims with their foreign creeds and denied them their own customs, languages and place names (not to mention their land and livelihoods!), such that many lost sight of the intrinsic worth of their indigenous culture and Country, and became second class citizens in it.

So much wisdom and harmony has been lost in the world in this way.

Invader cultures have been mostly blind to the exquisite beauty of native vegetation in their colonies, too. In Australia, native fauna and flora extinctions are barely mourned while people living in the temperate regions of the south still aspire to an English country style garden, despite lacking adequate rainfall. Left to its own devices, nature is usually able to maintain it's own sacred balance of plants and animals in a landscape. But colonial introductions throw the wildlife totally out of whack. In Australia plagues of rabbits, plus foxes, cats and the like have devastated landscapes, which struggle to regenerate, choked with feral plants. European style agriculture has also destroyed Australian landscapes, spoiling in just two centuries what the indigenous management beforehand maintained over many millennia.

As a devout animist and Land Lover, to help recapture what has been lost I always aim for a high level of indigenousness in my permaculture design. That means my first choice of a plant to fulfil a function, wherever possible, is a native, locally endemic species.

Sacred sites across the world have also been trashed by invading peoples, who quickly appropriated them for their own purposes of propaganda and domination. Rarely have existing cultural and spiritual traditions been left alone by colonising forces, normally intent on total control of the population and lands for the plundering of resources.

Mythos has become rather confused in the process. Thus are added to some place stories ugly episodes of local goddesses being raped or sidelined by the new mob of invading gods/ saints/ heroes, such that are the favourites of the new order. But don't believe all the pseudo-history and pseudo mythos that was cooked up. Those old gods and goddesses are still out there and they retain great powers!

These days colonisation is more subtle and sometimes it feels like we are all being herded along, subsumed into a single, bland and paranoid new world order. Foreign domination can come from economic warfare, with huge transnational companies the most powerful players of them all. To quote Michael Moore – 'Hey dude, who owns your country?' And farmer activists might ask - 'Who controls the crop seeds on your farm?'

In view of all this, we barely recognise that what we see and interpret of the world is filtered through our cultural interpretation and expectations, which can be subject to collective manipulation (such as religion), while our personal experiences also colour our world of perception. So how unbaggaged is our awareness when we look around us? Do we see with understanding or with habit? Are we blind to what is there in front of our eyes? Can we grasp the beauty and spirit of a place directly, or do we slavishly follow established ways of thinking and perceiving? I suggest we really need to loosen up and be open to whatever is out there. And it may not always be nice!

Unwelcoming lands

Donegal artist Marion Rose MacFadden grew up in a Gaelic speaking part of north west Ireland and was well immersed in the Celtic spirit and traditions. She is a painter of wild landscapes and the spirits of place of her homeland. But she doesn't romanticise these places.

"Those bare mountainsides, all rocky or boggy. They're so infertile. Most of the original inhabitants never chose those marginal lands. They were refugees, forced to move into the western fringes because of wars and 'plantation' [herded there from Ulster when it was 'planted' with Scottish Protestants] and it was a very hard life for them. Very few could survive there at the best of times and it had previously been pretty much uninhabited," she told me.

This reminded me how, in most parts of Australia, Aboriginal peoples' lands were stolen, they were denied their sovereignty and forced to live in mixed-clan reservations. These were on the poorest lands of all, where they were not able to subsist as hunter-gatherers. Not surprisingly, they often cursed their homelands as they were dragged away, often in chains, as the only thing left in their power to do in protest.

To this day certain areas are avoided by Aboriginal people, due to the awful history or cursed energy there. I wonder if the so-called 'cursing' stones sometimes found at ancient Irish monuments were once used for this purpose, by people similarly suffering terrible injustices?

"Some people like to come here now," Marion continued, "and they say how they love the stark, bare beauty of the landscape, the coastal mountains and glens. They want to settle where a lot of sad history has gone down. But those places are more misery than beauty. They think they can just have a little ceremony or something to make it okay. But the place doesn't want them and they never prosper. They make out they are sensitive, but they don't listen to what the land is saying, when it's telling them to just go away!"

"There are so many really sad places, but people think they can make them better, when really it's all too hard and they are best out of there," she said.

I wasn't surprised to hear all this. I know that people bring their own energies to places and strong emotions and forceful thoughts become enmeshed in the Akasha Records, from where they can infect or haunt a place. Like tends to attract like and more strong emotion can be generated as different people are subconsciously attracted by those energies and often proceed to enact out the memories lurking there (such as violence, suicide and murder).

The Irish landscape is a painfully haunted one. Stories from the Great Irish Famine times speak of untold suffering. Whole families in pitiful one room hovels died of starvation and disease, while fat landlords averted their gaze. People today are disinclined to go near, let alone demolish the crumbling ruins of these homes that may well be still harbouring a heavy emotional load one hundred and fifty odd years later.

Fortunately, being biodegradable, the stone walled ruins are mouldering back to the elements and we can allow nature to reclaim them. We can simply leave them be. Or if the space is needed for redevelopment, ceremonial space healing may be required. This can be an opportunity for past traumas to be ritually acknowledged and energetically released, and for positive new ch'i to be invited in to replace the old.

In geomantic analysis we need to discover any emotional place memories and also be aware of the energies we ourselves bring to a place. Often it is our own self that needs to change before any energetic space clearing is possible. Everything is inter-connected, so to attain, regain or maintain environmental harmony requires honesty and clarity. We may well have to be a part of the ongoing fix that is required.

Learning to listen

Peeling back our awareness we can learn to listen intently to the land and to our own hearts. What is stopping us from achieving a good relationship with a place? Do we also have a good relationship with ourselves and with others? Or are we just acting as a controller of our environment and our kindred? The urge to gain power over others underlies the Western way, underpinning the unsustainable capitalist system.

Some people, on the other hand, go the other extreme and give up their own power in dabbling with their psychic abilities and channelling information from potentially dubious sources in the spirit world. They usually become quite ungrounded in the process and what they write tends to be predictable warnings and advice. Some interesting information has been gained in this manner, but there are also trickster spirits giving supposedly 'spiritual guidance' that's fairly worthless. Some people call up the nature spirits and expect them to do as they bid. This might be rather patronising to the devas, I suspect.

Per-Uno Franssen, a dowser and clairvoyant colleague in Sweden, thinks that many people aspiring to interact with the devas may just be deluding themselves. The only sure form of communication, he says, is that which is two-way. In other words, we need to be listening to what the devas are saying or asking of us. He is involved with an organisation – 'Helping the Earth' - which has as one of its aims that of helping the devas to cope with the challenges of the modern world. (I have put a short film about this – 'Helping the Devas'- up at You Tube.)

Only when communication with the devas is two-way can we know that we are listening properly and also being listened to. This could also be said for human communications, which seem to get sketchier all the time, especially when reduced to texting and other rapid and truncated forms. 'Improving' technologies don't necessarily mean that human communications are improving at all!

We may encounter unfriendly energies and beings in the Dreaming fabric of places and we need to respect the fact that humans are not always welcome to just come and go everywhere as they please. If a place is not welcoming to us, we need to avoid it. Sometimes being patient, we may be eventually allowed in and there may be a right time for this to happen. But better to put our own precious energies into the places where we will be welcomed and our efforts more easily fruitful, I think.

These days the rich heritage of Irish and Australian indigenous, pre-Christian cultural landscapes and customs is fading rapidly, with most people disinterested in land lore. Sacred sites are languishing, unkempt or erased. The wisdom keepers - such as Aboriginal elders and Irish seanchaí storytellers - are dying out.

But we can always reverse the trend and become wisdom keepers ourselves. A revolution in consciousness is needed! We need to wake up and realise that we have all been sleeping giants in the landscape. The Earth can be held sacred again, be helped and be fruitful.

All that's required is a good plan.

The Irish Famine sculpture at Carrick-on-Shannon, Co. Leitrim, was a depressing sight until Alanna did some 'guerilla' planting of flowers into it. This event will be the subject of Alanna's next You Tube film.

Chapter 6: Assessing land capability

'A piece of land is like a piece of gold.'
Vietnamese saying.

Path of least effort

All land has intrinsic value. But sometimes it needs viewing with much creative vision to discover how we can get the most out of it. When selecting land, if you know what you are looking for in relation to a permaculture lifestyle, no matter how unattractive or un-fertile that land may seem, there is always something useful you can do with it and something that will grow there. You can make just about any place beautiful and productive.

Taking the sensible Path of Least Effort, a cornerstone of permaculture design, it is better to find out what will prosper there without too much fuss or alteration and to select what will fit in with the general capability of that site. Look around at what neighbours are doing with their land and see which plants and animals are thriving nearby.

Too often people hastily buy some inappropriate land for its superficial qualities and then have to make so many changes to it that the expense involved is way out of proportion to any yields produced. This is usually the insensitive approach.

A load of money is often spent rapidly before enough time has elapsed to really think things out properly. Expensive mistakes can easily be made. Especially when workers are hired and they have different sets of values when working the land. So it's better to find land that fits your general plan.

Ethics of site selection

Many people in Australia fall in love with forested areas where they buy land covered in beautiful trees. They then have to cut the trees down to accommodate their homes and insurance policies, or face the unnerving threat of fire hazard, particularly in highly flammable forests, such as pine and eucalypt. Buying a bush block to live amidst nature and then proceeding to hack nature back seems to me to be defeating the whole purpose of being there.

The reality behind the romance of a bush setting is tempered by having to suffer vegetable garden raids from forest wildlife. Tree roots, also, rob gardens of moisture and nutrients. On my farm in Victoria the big Yellow Gums send roots out up to 50 metres in the search for sustenance in the hard, dry ground there, after 14 years of drought. There is no point planting any vegetable beds in contact with the soil there, only container growing works in the long term.

People love to play God with topography and because big machines can move anything and change everything so quickly, this may not be a very ethical approach. The spirits of place may become totally traumatised and this can place an unnerving taint on the atmosphere. It may be especially risky to play with hydrology too. Diverting streams or draining bogs from around your dream home site may have repercussions. Waters may return to haunt you.

Mankind has been 'at war with topography' (as John Pilger described of the Vietnam war) for too long. I think we owe it to the Earth to take a more gentle, caring approach to our custodianship of Her. Rather than buying land that we have to ravage to suit our will, it's more sustainable, I think, to concentrate on finding the most suitable piece of land for what we intend to do.

Recovering landscapes

"Better to buy a bare, degraded bit of land and to restore it back to fertility" is the mantra of Junitta Vallak, who took up the challenge herself and revegetated 100 acres of wasted farm land in central Victoria. 'Casurina' was, for many years, a focal point for eco-spirituality and geomantic work associated with the 'Renewing of the Dreaming' movement and Native American Sun Dances in the 1980's-90's. These days, her work done, Junitta has moved on and Casurina is now just a private property (and a haven for wildlife).

Back in the 1980s it was also in the state of Victoria that the popular Landcare movement of Australia was born. This facilitates farmers and landholders to work together co-operatively to revegetate whole catchments, creating wildlife corridors that cross boundaries to link up remnant vegetation, and assisting each other to restore degraded farmlands. Their work is vital not only for wildlife, but also for stream water quality and even the long term sustainability of farming. Farmers need all the help they can get to reverse soil degradation and keep producing food in more sustainable ways. Human communities are thus also enriched in the Landcare process.

Patterns of influence

The permaculture approach to assessing land capability is to start by finding out just what the intrinsic characteristics of the land are. To do this well one ideally makes careful observations over the course of all the seasons of the year, monitoring patterns of light, wind and water movement.

* Is enough sunlight available, or is the aspect too shady?

* What range of temperatures and rainfall could be expected over the course of the year, statistics of which should be available from meteorological bureaux. (Localised climate can be somewhat variable to such stats and neighbours are best consulted for accurate local weather know-how.)

* Are there any frosts and how does the site's topography affect frost incidence?

* If there are great views in a high elevation, what is it like on a windy day? 'Where there's a view, there's a wind,' is the way it goes!

While your assessment of land capability is underway you also need to identify any potential hazards lurking there.

* If the land is flat, is it subject to flooding from a nearby water way, or poor drainage?

* How often do droughts occur and and are water catchments diverse and sufficient to sustain you over dry spells?

Neighbours can be helpful for tapping into site histories and local council records may also assist.

State of the soil

It's also wise to discover the state of the soil at your chosen site, ideally before taking the purchasing plunge. If you are starting out with degraded farmland to restore – a most noble occupation! – you may be inheriting leached out, poisoned or dead soils. Good soils on farms usually end up being stripped of minerals and essential elements after years of cropping.

Find out if the soil is either clay, loam or sand based. (Different areas of the land may well have different soil types too.) Clay based soils can be very fertile, but drainage can be a problem. (You can add gypsum powder and organic matter to improve them.) Whilst being very well drained, sandy soils are less fertile and need added organic matter (or even clay) to improve fertility. Loamy soils are a mixture between the two and can be ideal.

Take a handful of top soil, add some water and knead it like dough to see if it sticks together. If it becomes sticky and glistening with a silky feeling, and if you can make a long thin ribbon of it - then it is a predominantly clay soil. Or put the soil sample in a jar half filled with water, shake it up and let it settle. The organic matter will float to the top and layering will reveal the constituents.

Testing for toxic chemical residues should definately be done before land is purchased, if land history suggests any probability. If DDT sprays were ever used, for instance, they linger for nobody-knows-how long and also create toxic breakdown daughter products that hang around in the soil for ages. Contaminated soils may take years to remediate (if ever!) and gain organic growing status. There are many ways to revive such soils - spreading basalt rock dust, organic mulching and covercropping are worthwhile.

It's good to also discover the pH level of the soil, its acidity or alkalinity levels, to understand how your soil might be behaving. Does it smell or taste sour, indicating acidity? Many old farm soils have been rendered highly acid from farm chemical applications, such as superphosphate. Low pH levels (too acid) can inhibit nitrogen, phosphorus or trace element levels and ideally the pH will be hovering around 6.5, which is about neutral. The raising of low pH levels with an application of lime can make previously unavailable elements become available to plants. Alternatively, an application of crushed basalt rock, which is highly alkaline and a waste product of gravel crushing, can sweeten sour soils in a slower, more gentle manner. (My book 'Stone Age Farming' focusses on the benefits of using this 'blue metal' rock.)

Generally speaking there are few soils that could be considered naturally perfect for growing nutrient rich food crops. Your choice of crops will dictate the range of nutrients requiring to be added to the soil. Ideally select plants that will want to grow in the overall conditions there, without too much alteration of soil conditions.

Soil dowsing

Soil analysis from a laboratory may be a good idea, but it can be expensive and might not always be accurate. You can always try soil testing by dowsing. Some master dowsers, like Tasmania's Ross Henderson, have developed great skill at soil testing this way and they can quickly and accurately assess soil mineral balance and pH levels of a sample. (You can see Ross undertaking a soil dowsing test in his garden, in my film 'Remineralising the Soil'.)

But if you are just a novice you might like to try soil dowsing and also send away the sample to a laboratory to double check. It's a great confidence booster for your dowsing if they agree. But then again, laboratories are not always accurate in terms of finding out what is potentially available to plants, only usually assessing what elements are found in a soluble state. Different systems and methods of soil testing abound and each can give different results. A study by the Weekly Times newspaper in Victoria a few years ago gained 18 different results from 18 different laboratories for the one sample!

With the dowsing approach, you might start by asking with your dowsing tool: 'Can I identify what is needed to add to this soil to make the selected crop grow to its optimum?' You might take your soil sample (and possibly crop samples too) to a farm store or rock crushing quarry and dowse over the various soil additives or rock dusts to see if any would suit. Going through the agricultural business section in the phone book seeking suitable suppliers by dowsing the listings might be usefully attempted. Dowsing saves time, money and energy and gets good results for many people.

Soil aeration and initial planting

Having purchased your dream land, while assessing all relevant factors over the first year you will no doubt have itchy feet and want to start working with it as soon as!

If soil is compacted from livestock and machinery, then one of the first jobs might ideally be deep ripping across the contours of your site, to loosen and aerate the soil. Hillsides thus ripped can harvest rainfall so much the better and if this is done across a whole catchment the tendency for waterways to flooding is greatly reduced, while soil moisture levels are much improved. Trees can subsequently be planted into the rip lines, saving the tree planters' energies. It's particularly good for areas of future treebelts and crops to be deep ripped before planting, possibly even cross ripping the ground in both directions.

Single tined rippers are okay, but it's better to use some of the smarter equipment available. For example, the Yeoman's Plow and other equipment produced in Australia by the Yeomans family, known for their acclaimed system of agricultural landscape rainwater harvesting - the Keyline system. Much flogged farm land has been restored to life purely by such sensitive aeration of the soil, where topsoil is not inverted, as in conventional ploughing and ripping.

After soil aeration, the next job to address might be the issue of any strong prevailing winds, with some astute tree planting to intercept them. Windbreak shelterbelts are wonderfully multi-purpose things. When treecover on farmland is returned, at up to around 30% of land area, it actually increases farm productivity and viability, studies have shown. Crops and livestock do much better with shelterbelts to protect them from extreme weather. Windbreaks can include useful or edible species. They might be planted in the form of traditional European hedgerows, for maximising wildlife habitat and biodiversity in small areas. Otherwise, for best effect, plant windbreaks across the path of prevailing winds, having at least five rows width of mixed shrubs and trees. Planting in clumps and groves, leaving gaps to allow for some wind permeability, is better than a solid wall of vegetation, which might itself create wind nuisance from turbulence.

Treebelts can also protect homes from firestorms that blow in, deflecting the fire-front away and reducing the possibility of ember attack on buildings. In the dreadful bushfires of February 2009 in Victoria, amidst several thousands of homes that were incinerated, some were left standing, saved by being surrounded by lush, permaculture-like gardens that had a dampening or deflecting effect on the fire.

At the earliest opportunity on your precious 'piece of gold', it's a perfect first step to do soil conditioning and start to establish windbreaks, if these are required. Transformation of the land will then be more easily achieved and more rapidly too.

Chapter 7: Geobiology and Geomancy

'Hungry grass'

On a grassy pathway on a hillside in Ireland a group of students gathered around me to watch as I dowsed the position of an underground stream of water. My pendulum spun around in rapid circles in response to the rising energy from the water's ch'i flow path. They then followed the example and soon more pendulums were also spinning as students walked across the zone. I then discovered a second line of energy crossing over the first and, as one would have expected, an energy vortex spinning downwards at the crossover point.

I showed them how, if one stood at that cross point your legs might begin to sag in sudden weakness from the detrimental, downward pulling effect. Long term exposure to this type of environmental energy, for people sleeping and animals and plants positioned over such a strong energy zone, can potentially be fatal.

One of the students, James Monahan, an experienced dowser himself, piped in. "That's what the old folks would call the *fear gortha*, the 'hungry grass'. They would put offerings at those points, out of fear of them," he told us. I was intrigued, as I'd read about the 'hungry grass' in a book about the Great Irish Famine. There were stories of people suffering terribly from starvation who, when unfortunate enough to linger a while over some 'hungry grass', would succumb to death rapidly. (Food, even just an oatcake, was said to be the cure for such exposure.) Offerings of crumbs of food would be left at such a dangerous spot in order to appease the fairies. So I was not surprised for James to make the noxious energy connection.

Elsewhere in Europe there has long been recognition of places that are deadly or dangerous to sleep over. People in the German speaking countries speak of 'cancer beds' and 'cancer streets'. The modern world now calls such places 'geopathic zones' and warns of the consequences of spending a lot of time where the geobiology of a place is unhealthy.

Geobiology denotes recognition of the biological effects that can result from subtle energetic influences. Geopathic stresses arise from a range of energies that emanate from below the ground. Scientific instrumentation can identify them, reading the changes to electrical ionisation and measuring unhealthy radiation emissions, such as microwaves, and other such factors in these zones. Dowsing is the usual method, however.

Geobiologists associate geopathic stress exposure with a range of distressed behaviours and dis-eases, such as insomnia , cancer (leukemias and lymphomas in particular), cot death, kids who never want to go to bed or who have learning difficulties, mental illness, fatigue, ME, endocrine dysfunction, heart problems, migraines, and all manner of conditions which fail to improve, no matter the treatment.

It is always wise to check out the geobiology of a place, especially if you feel uncomfortable, irritable or often very tired there. You might try by dowsing with the question – 'Is any geopathic stress here that could detrimentally affect me?' If you do find some, best to avoid it! Move furniture or move rooms. If you can't avoid it, Earth acupuncture and other neutralising techniques can be employed. You might also save lives by telling others about this!

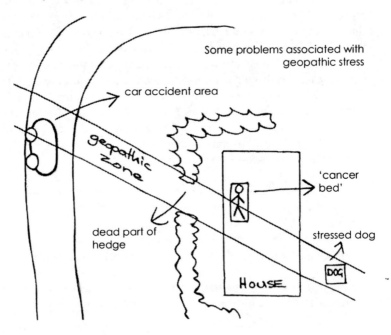

Some problems associated with geopathic stress

car accident area

geopathic zone

dead part of hedge

'cancer bed'

stressed dog

DOG

HOUSE

Geomancy and Earth dragons

The geobiology of today was the geomancy of yesterday. But geomancy is also much more. Originally the term had a different meaning and it referred to a form of Arabic divination. In modern usage, however, geomancy refers to the art of reading the landscape for its subtle energies and spirit presences, our relationship with Earth's sacred centres and cosmic connections as well.

The oldest traditions of geomancy are those of the Australian Aboriginal peoples. The animist Aboriginal view of nature, of its Dreaming and spirit, is very similar to the ancient European, and other global perceptions that have elsewhere faded or died out over the last few centuries. However geomancy remains a living tradition in the Australian Aboriginal community.

In northern Australian mythos, for example, the primary creator of landscape features is the great Rainbow Serpent, who also has lesser, localised manifestations. Like other forms of wildlife, such serpent spirits inhabit particular landscape features (usually watery places), keeping to themselves, getting on with their lives and being protective of their homes. Rainbow Serpents play much the same role as the dragons spirits of Chinese, Asian, European and other cultures.

A Rainbow Serpent features in the permaculture logo that describes the wholistic paradigm of permaculture design. Its body forms a circle, the end of its tail in its mouth, to denote the cyclic characteristics of nature and climate. Bill Mollison in the preface to his biblical tome, the 'Permaculture Designers Manual', informs us that Aboriginal people strongly believe that the Earth is totally sacred and that the Rainbow Serpent is not to be disturbed in its underground home. Other traditions, such as feng shui, are also concerned with such issues.

Sacred sites can be likened to human chakra points that help to distribute life enhancing forces throughout the landscape. They are often found where Earth energies are most intense and feature a concentration of nature spirits. Looking regionally in a wholistic approach to archaeology, 'ritual landscapes' of associated sacred sites are recognised for their connectedness. This mirrors clairvoyant and dowsing observations of energetic connections between sacred sites. It has been

41

observed that columns of light often reach up to the sky from such sites (also from certain mountain tops) and that these connect into aerial energy ley systems (also incorrectly called ley lines) in star-like patterns, like an etheric spiderweb in the air. So problems at one site might affect others and, conversely, energy healing work done there may radiate out to a larger area from these places of divine Earth spirit.

Planning with the fairies

Ancient peoples the world over have long recognised the nature beings of the spiritual dimensions of landscape. Denied recognition in most mainstream religions, today the devic presences are being reaffirmed as a new generation of sensitive people, including dowsers, confirm their existence.

The Indian term 'deva' is often used as a general name for the various types of nature spirit, including the gods and goddesses. Clairvoyants tell us what the devas look like and clairaudients receive messages from them. Dowsers can interview them, gaining yes or no answers to dowsed questions. The highly evolved devic beings may use more sophisticated telepathy for direct communication.

Traditional stories everywhere reinforce the idea of respecting the devas and keeping them happy. As nature spirits tend to congregate at certain topographic, energetic and vegetative features of the landscape, it behoves the sensitive developer to initially check the site for devic centres and to minimise any disturbance to them.

There may even be a legal requirement to do this. In 2006 came news from Perthshire, Scotland, of a land developers plans being thwarted by the locals, who insisted that a large stone he wanted removed was the sacrosanct home of the fairies! Scottish geomancer and author David Cowan was interviewed for television at the site, after which, he told me, he left an offering on the stone, placing a coin inside a cup-and-ring mark carving on it.

Afterwards other people also started to leave offerings. A pile of money soon stacked up. The developer had to go back to the drawing board and design around the stone. Folkloric traditions of the land have legally protected status in that part of the world.

In Irish country mythos is found a treasure trove of fairy wisdom and the old stories should not be dismissed. They give us clues for how to work sensitively with the land. James Monahan gave my dowsing class another tip.

"The old people used to put out buckets of water at the four corners of where they planned their home to be built. If these were spilled, then it was believed this would cause upset to the fairies and they'd have to choose another site", he explained.

I've also heard of similar traditions - placing a pile of stones at each corner of the building site, or digging the foundations and then waiting a few days to see if anything was disturbed.

Lady Gregory wrote around one hundred years ago of an Irish healer called Fagan, who they said was given 'second sight' and 'the cure' from his dead sister. He was a "great warrior in this business and no man within miles of the place will build a house or a cabin or any other thing without him going there to say if it's in a right place," she was told. Fagan was well known for consulting with the fairies on healing, as well as on building matters.

Whatever the mode, the approach is clear. We need to get 'planning permission' from the devas in order to live in true harmony with a place.

Feng shui

Feng shui, at a basic level, is the Chinese art of understanding the energetic patterns of landscape and buildings. Finding the best location, alignment and orientation for a house of the living or dead was the original preoccupation of feng shui masters. The hsueh, or ideal house site where beneficial ch'i accumulates, was calculated by landform observations and directional calculations made using a lo p'an compass.

These days the art has become very popular and commercialised. Esteemed author of feng shui books Stephen Skinner warns us that "a whole range of Chinese cultural trinkets and beliefs are now associated in the Western mind with feng shui [when they] are not a part of traditional feng shui." He notes that this is also true for interior décor, clutter clearing, dowsing and geopathic stress etc. And feng shui has also, Skinner adds, "nothing to do with ecology."

That said, feng shui has had a long track record (3000 years or so) in determining harmonious home sites, where people prosper and are fruitful down the generations. It's all location, location, location!

The ideal hsueh has been poetically described as 'the breath of the dragon arising from its nostrils'. Dragon veins (lung mai) bring ch'i down from mountain ranges to such a ch'i node. Hsueh is also translated as a den or cave, as well as an acupuncture point. In such nested nooks one might even get to see "the mist which often gathers at such hollows soon after dawn," as Skinner observed. Such ideal sites can often be found tucked into little pockets on hill or mountainsides, these being protected from strong or cold winds. But we don't always have such classically perfect landforms to work with. On a less grand scale, a good alternative backdrop can be a large tree, treebelt, grove or earth berm, if space allows.

Confirming the best home site

Everything hinges on there being a suitable house site available on your dream land site. So it's important to find out the appropriateness of a chosen house site before purchasing the land. By dowsing one may ask: 'Will it be okay with the Earth energies and spirits of place if I build my home just here?'

Hsueh sites, with gatherings of fecund energies, would be ideal for the home vegetable garden too, one surmises. But you need to be careful not to tread on the dragon's toes! If you do get the okay, you might want to ask similar questions of your plans for other areas. The simple act of asking can lead to all sorts of understandings and foster the ongoing development of a sensitive site plan.

After that you will need to make a more indepth site analysis to flesh out details and make the most of your 'piece of gold'.

Chapter 8: Sensitive site analysis

Connecting to the Dreaming

If we awaken to and respect its Dreaming qualities, the magic of the land can be accessible to us. By connecting to the energies and intelligences of a place, by allowing it to speak to us and co-operating with it, rather than just imposing our will upon it, we can co-create a better world for all. When we act this way, as I've found myself, the harmony just flows! Obstructions dissolve, relationships prosper and life is filled with serendipity.

So how to begin the site analysis? At the very beginning of a sensitive permaculture design process you need to walk the land slowly, in an open and respectful state of being. Perambulate the boundaries. Pay attention to any odd or unusual occurrences, as the old feng shui masters would do. These might carry special portence, conveying symbolic meaning to be intuited.

Where does the place feel special, or nicely energetic? Sites of intense energy must be treated with care, ideally never to be built upon or disturbed. They can make ideal wilderness zones, perfect for wildlife and the devas. Or you might want to delineate and protect them with special stone arrangements and use them as your own sacred sites.

Microclimates

Select the ideal home site and the rest of the plan can radiate out from there. Ideal feng shui for the home site would be to have a protective hill,

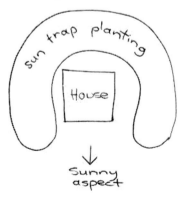

dense shelterbelt of trees, artificial earthberm or line of buildings behind the house site. This would be to the north, in the northern hemisphere, or to the south in the southern hemisphere. Around such a home a sun-trap effect can thus be created as an excellent micro-climate for Zone One and Two gardens.

In passive solar house design living areas are located to face the sun (except, of course, in very hot climates). This is a very different criteria to the typical suburban home, which is normally built to face the street. Planning laws are more concerned with conformity to the norm. But if a home can at least have it's back to the sunny aspect, then passive solar gain can be harnessed there (such as by attaching hot houses for food growing) without upsetting streetscapes.

Across the whole site you will need to observe patterns of sun, wind and water and see how the topography alters these to create localised microclimates. Altitude will affect temperatures, with cold air sinking down into valley floors, creating frost hollows, making a hillside the warmer location. But in colder climates, where snow falls on hilltops and not below, the valleys might be warmer. Hilltops might be the sunniest of places, but winds may well make it chilly up there in winter.

Don't worry if your site is bare. In fact this makes it easier for earthmoving equipment and general access. In fact I think it's better to have land that is a 'blank slate', where your landscaping can create something far better, over time, than having to undo or dodge what others have done before you.

Survey the wildlife

Find out which wild animals are also residing on your site or nearby. Where are birds nesting or any large animals living or hibernating? Protect them from inappropriate development. Will nearby woodlands be a source of animals, such as deer or kangaroos, which may be intent on eating your garden? You may need to budget for some good fencing.

Discover the wildlife by their scats (manure) and tracks. Animal tracks might make good pathways for people and keeping them intact will help keep everyone happy. Some animals, such as deer, have been found by dowsers to follow particular energetic pathways.

Trackways

In the early 20th century English dowser Guy Underwood discovered energy lines that co-incided with pathways of human movement. We know today that peoples repeated movements leave behind an energy trail, so Underwood's observation was probably more of an result than a cause, in terms of the selection of a particular pathway. An effect of energetic slipstreams is that they may well facilitate movement themselves. You can always ask, by dowsing, if the energy of a track might be useful to you personally. There are also non-beneficial ones out there.

In old Ireland, Scotland and other places funeral processions always took a special route to the cemetery, so that the spirits of the newly deceased might not pass too close to the homes of the living and thus avoiding the possibility of them hanging around and haunting a place. David Cowan has written much about these 'spirit paths' and he has an informative website.

Dowser James Monahan told us about one such spirit path that runs across his farm in County Galway. There is even a special resting place for a coffin to sit on top of the stone field boundary fence, to help them cross over the style. "When my folks had a horse for ploughing it would always refuse to plough that field, where the spirit path crossed. Spooked it would be," he said.

The Irish are so very intuitive and traditionally they had a close relationship with the land. They recognised energetic pathways that acted as road ways for the nature spirits (the 'Good People') to easily move along, in travels around their territory. Such 'fairy passes' can be found running between the old 'fairy forts'. Structures also known as raths or lios, these are typically the remains of Iron Age habitations and are found in great numbers across the country. They consist of circular earth and stone walled enclosures inside of which homes and livestock were once kept safe at night from marauding wolves and human raiders. But regular warfare meant that many people were killed in their rath homes and a reputation for being haunted places developed after they were abandoned. Thus being largely left alone until this day, it is not surprising that they became the wild refuges of nature and also the nature spirits, and that fairies would have well worn energetic pathways connecting them together. I imagine that the 'fairy trackways' could have been created as an energetic consequence of the fairies' movements.

Fairy passes must always be respected and never built over or disturbed, in numerous Irish fairy stories that warn us of such dangers. Some old

Irish homes are even oddly shaped, with cut off corners to accommodate the fairy passes. Homes unwisely built across these paths were expected to suffer misfortune or annoyances, such as finding front and back doors constantly opening mysteriously to allow for the passage of the fairies.

Vegetation mapping

'Under gorse there's gold, under rushes is silver and under heather there's poverty,' goes an old saying. Thus the Irish peasantry undertook a rough land assessment.

Likewise today, a study of existing vegetation can be very revealing. Existing plants give us clues to rainfall, wind strength and direction, and soil fertility. Some plants specialize in covering eroded, degraded sites. Others reveal the state of the soil, by their preference for soil with concentrations or deficiencies of particular nutrients. For example, Nettles indicate a phosphorus rich, fertile soil.

When the Surveyor for South Australia had to establish a demarcation point between arable country and the semi-arid north, to discourage any moves to settle land for cropping where it was too dry, he established the 'Goyder Line' by keen observation of the vegetation, which changed abruptly to semi-arid species at a certain latitude. Those farmers who ventured further north beyond the Goyder Line, emboldened by several years of good rain to grow abundant wheat crops, were only to be ruined by years of drought that followed.

In undertaking an initial plant survey, should you discover some rare or special native vegetation, this needs to be protected and it may well be a perfect area for a Zone Five wilderness. If feral weeds are infesting a native plant area you would ideally start to weed them out by hand slowly and carefully. Start at the best native part and work out to the most weedy. Thus is the basic strategy of the Bradley Method of Bush Regeneration. This was developed in Sydney, where serious weed infestations that choke many areas of bushland include blackberries and Scotch broom, those familiar plants the white settlers brought out to remind them of home. The Bradley sisters inspired a generation of voluntary bush regenerators, myself included, to go out and clean, weed and protect rapidly degrading native bushland in and around the city.

Chapter 9: Harmonising your space

Balance of the elements

In the ancient tenets of feng shui, to foster environmental harmony one strives for a balance of the elemental forces on one's land. On its most basic level this means one would first be looking at the balance of yin and yang; yin energy being calm and soothing, while yang energy is more stimulating.

Yang landscape features are high or rugged, with waterways that are fast flowing. Plains, hollows and still lakes are more on the yin side. The perfect balance of yin/yang, says feng shui, is to have three parts yang to two parts yin, thus - a bit more on the stimulating side.

Too much yang is dangerous and one should avoid living at the foot of a steep cliff, which is a very yang feature. Dangers of rock fall would be an obvious one. A very flat site would be considered too yin and rather dull. It would call for a yang feature, such as a towering pagoda, to be built, to stimulate the sluggish energy.

Then there are the elemental forces. In western thought only four elements are considered, being air, water, earth and fire. However I think it sensible to be more like the Chinese and include a fifth element, that of wood, which traditionally represents vegetation and growth in springtime. You might as well have a sixth element of metal too, another element that you don't want too much of.

How might you balance these elements? Try to compensate for missing elements and avoid any overbearing ones. For example, a bare site that has been totally cleared is crying out for the wood element to be restored, so you can plant trees and vegetation. A mountain top might have too much of the air element and be too windy to put your home there, while an underground home may well be too earthy. An all-steel home can make you angry, depressed and accident prone, reported the American Dowsers Quarterly Digest, spring 2005. But balancd with a lot of earthen or organic materials - bad efffects may be reduced.

Too much water in the landscape? Holland is a good example, being flat, watery and much below sea level. This situation can be very yin and calls for some fire energy, which is yang. A good way to pull in some yang fire energy is to erect a Tower of Power, which emits a stimulating energy field. A pagoda would be a more traditional resolution.

Sacred relationships with nature

For countless millennia humankind has developed sacred relationships with plants and animals, particularly those species associated with food or shelter. Trees have been held in special reverence and sacred lore proclaims them to be the wisdom keepers of the environment. Tree spirits were recognized for their sagacity and communicated with most reverently, especially the older specimens. Certain trees and their spirits (also known as dryads or fauns) became renowned as oracles. The prophetic Oak at Greece's Sacred Grove of Dodona is a good example. Here pilgrims converged for over 2000 years, up until the 4th century BCE. The sounds of rustling Oak leaves and the gushing of springwater from the Oak's base were interpreted by priestesses who were consulted for sometimes highly important matters of state.

Plant devas have also communicated important knowledge of plant medicine to shamanic healers the world over. This helps to explain the wealth of plant knowledge from ancient times. To gain all that information, the healers couldn't just have guessed, or used trial and error, which would have sometimes proved fatal! Lady Gregory was told about this around 100 years ago in the west of Ireland. The Irish healers of old, she wrote, when gathering the healing herbs, would "call upon the 'king' or 'queen' of the plant", in other words the plant deva, for direct assistance. The famous Irish psychic healer Biddy Early was said to have gained her know-how 'directly from the fairies', which no doubt included plant devas.

Gaining knowledge directly from the plant kingdom is possible for anyone curious enough to try. You don't have to be 'gifted'. Allow your intuition to be your guide. By dowsing you might simply pose questions to a plant, where the answer can either be yes or no. It's good manners to respectfully introduce yourself first, of course, and to ask if there's something the plant would like to communicate. Talk to the plants on your site and be receptive to what they might have to say to you. The best times for this type of questing is usually when you have a strong need-to-know something, or dowse for when would be a suitable time.

The bleakness of degraded landscapes might be brought back to harmony by also introducing livestock. Animals bring an emotional gift to a place. Happy animals bringing joyful richness can introduce a vibrant, yang element. It will get you moving too, criss-crossing the land to check on their welfare, you become more animated yourself.

However I suggest you think deep and long before taking the plunge, as going away for holidays gets much more complicated when animals have to be minded. And have a low enough stocking rate that you won't have big feed bills at certain times of the year. Cute animal lawn mowers can become expensive liabilities when the grass is not growing. Think twice also, before introducing any cloven hooved animals that can slice up soft soil and trash stream banks, as is the case all over Ireland, Australia and elsewhere. Dowsing your soil for toxins may also be a good idea, to check its suitability for pasture, as toxins dumped in some areas include arsenic from gold mining, DDT from sheep dips, CCA from timber treatment plants and the like.

Alanna's llamas are quiet and soft footed.

51

While usually bringing a loving energy to a place, normally happy animal behaviour can change if they are exposed to hazardous electro-magnetic radiation, such as from a nearby radar station. Animal wellbeing can be disrupted and health disturbed, with males becoming particularly aggressive, while fertility is generally lost, reports Powerwatch UK. So discover if any high tech installations in the district are impacting on your site. Phone mast locations for Australia are available on-line and Google Earth's all-seeing eye might also be consulted.

Sometimes neighbours may be blind to welfare issues and keep unhappy animals in cages, where they stew with frustration. This creates an atmosphere of bad vibes (and unhappy noises) that can spill out over onto your own land. I once had a consultancy job where the people had nurtured a lovely space in their own backyard, but it was spoiled at times by the noisy animals kept by the nasty neighbour, who also harboured grudges against them. (The concept of the Evil Eye is very real. It can come from someone's bad thoughts about you, from envy or grumpiness.)

In that case I could only suggest placing mirrors (the 'aspirin' of feng shui) along the boundary, in order to reflect back what was being sent out energetically.

Hauntings and emotional debris

Sometimes people find themselves in homes that make them feel sick, over-emotional or uncomfortable, and it is not because of geopathic stress. Learning something of the house history they might discover that this is a pattern that has been recurring for some time. Strong emotions, especially from violence, deep sadness or depression, can linger in the energetic fabric of a place. Emotional debris and thoughtforms from past residents are a force to be reckoned with!

There can even be a subconscious attraction to such places and if we want harmony in the home we need to work out what and why it is. Couples moving into such a place can have their relationship severely put to the test. Fortunately, if identified in time, adjustments and improvements can be made. These could be in the form of meditation and the visualisation of cleansing and healing colours circulating around the rooms. Bells might be rung ritually in every corner. A lively house warming party and interior redecoration may also be worthwhile. Whatever the mode, project thoughtforms of love, joy and harmony in the process of space healing.

As for haunted places, usually it's just emotional fragments of people that may be lingering behind. Sending love to these astral fragments and asking them to move on to the light, where their loved ones are waiting for them, can be a good idea. But ask the Universe if this is permissable first. In some cultures the expectation is for the spirits of the dead to permanently inhabit their territory, watching over family and clanspeople and offering help and guidance where needed.

This has been a universal concept and vibrant today still in Aboriginal Australia, where peoples' spirits are said to go back to the sacred sites from where their mothers received them in the first place. Similarly, from ancient Ireland comes the tradition that the Tuatha da Danaan tribe were said to have gone to ground, disappearing into the 'fairy mounds' after losing a decisive territorial battle. It turns out that thousands of years previously these mounds (also known as passage graves) were the monuments where kings (tribal chieftains) were buried and their descendents crowned upon. From the ancestral soul soup gestating in these mounds, new spirits were probably once thought to have emerged, as icons found inside some of these womb-like monuments are obvious fertility symbols.

A site of a battle or massacre will often feature disturbed energies that may be totally unworkable and not fit for living beings. These need the hand of nature to mellow them down vegetatively and energetically. Traditionally the 'haunted' sites of Ireland are left to moulder in the elements, in the process becoming de facto Zone Five wilderness areas.

Because of this Ireland has more ancient monuments surviving that what has remained in all of Europe. But relatively little archeological work has been done and that's probably fortunate, as archeologists have a record for trashing sites that they excavate. Irish archeology is notoriously insensitive, with 'restoration' and repairs of priceless monuments using concrete and steel being energetically and aesthetically damaging.

Earth acupuncture

Where points or lines of energy are causing geopathic stress in the home and can't be avoided, then Earth acupuncture might be used to relieve the problem. This can be a means to release stagnant energy and allow the Earth to 'breathe' better.

But always ask for Universal permission. Too much gung ho space clearing can upset the spirits of place. For instance water lines, which are the energy flows above underground streams, are favourite places for water spirits, who love to play and work with the energies there. Who are we to neutralise the energy and make them homeless, especially if it is not totally necessary to do so, such as in the garden? Treat the energies as intelligent and tell them what you have in mind to do, so you can better understand the repercussions of your plan.

A copper pipe or wooden stake (or several) are typically used for this type of land treatment. This is combined with the force of intentions and the appropriateness of the point being needled, all determined, of course, by dowsing. Some people then remove the stake, otherwise it's left in the ground as a permanent fixture. Other geomancers specialize in effecting remote energy corrections at a distance.

Trees can also be positioned as a sort of acupuncture treatment, planted to improve the feng shui by balancing the elements and providing invigoration to low energy sites. Some species are also very good at intercepting hazardous radiation from high tech installations. Other trees, however, are badly affected by radiation and forest dieback can sometimes be seen to occur in lines between radio and military transmitters, or along geopathic stress zones.

So carefully select which trees to plant if radiations are beaming hazardously at you from the local mobile phone mast, radar station, tv/radio transmitters and the like. Some tree species planted to intercept beams will able to screen people, pets or livestock to some degree, eucalyptus species being a good example.

For protecting homes from electro-magnetic-radiation there are also plug-in devices and a type of paint, developed by the Germany military, that can be painted on as an undercoat beneath normal house paint.

Altering energy patterns

Other types of natural energy that impinge on places can potentially be cleared or shifted in different ways. Some energies can be tricky, however. Be careful if you have a big dragon line or vortex in the house. Strong energies cannot always simply be cast out!

You might offer the energy an alternative location to be moved to. When all augurs well for this to happen, a new spot can be dowsed for and a little ceremony conducted, with energies respectfully asked to move to the new location.

I'll give an example of how I have done this. I was asked by one of the architects to dowse the site for a new kindergarten building at Canberra's Steiner School. On the plan I detected a strong energy vortex in the middle of the building site. This would potentially cause disruption in the classroom. (The younger those afflicted, the more vulnerable they are.)

Unfortunately there was not enough room to re-position the building away from that spot. When I had a chance to visit the site in person, together with clairvoyant Billy Arnold, I soon found the big vortex. I talked to it and explained what was planned for the site, showing it, by visualisation, the future scenario. Better for all if it would move to another spot, I respectfully suggested.

I dowsed for an alternative location for the vortex, finding a suitable spot well away from the building site. There I dug a little hole and placed a few nice little stones in it. Thus prepared, I went back to the vortex, attuned into resonance with it, with a short meditation, and asked if it would now move with me to the new location. By dowsing it indicated that yes, it was ready to move.

With a little amethyst crystal held on my outstretched hand I started to walk, very slowly, towards the new spot. As I did this I could feel a wave of energies moving with me. Afterwards Billy, who had been watching, told me that he had clairvoyantly observed the vortex, as well as a host of nature spirits, moving slowly along with me as I walked. At the new vortex spot I buried the amethyst crystal and little stones, thanking the energies for their co-operation. The work was done and it all felt good.

Honour the spirit beings

Apart from the usual geomantic structures in the landscape (lines, points and zones of energy), I find that devas may also have a strong influence on a site. The sensitive developer will discover who the local devas of place are and whether they are happy about what is being planned.

However, as humans don't have a good environmental track record in the devas minds, they will probably be wary of you (and they are terrified of bulldozers!). So you need to make gentle contact, gauge their mood and offer a loving hand of co-operation to them.

Working together, humans and devas have a great capacity to co-create a better world for all. But most devas will have had no beneficial contact with humans and may need extra reassurance that they and their homes will be safe. You can dowse where they are stationed and 'interview' them by dowsing. Asking, as always, for their permission first!

James Monahan told us a story of a woman who longed to live in the isolated wilderness of an Irish bog, on land where people may never have lived before. She had built a timber house on stilts, trying to make as minimal an environmental impact as possible. But her dreams of idyllic peace and quiet were hampered by a feeling of unease. It just didn't feel right there.

"She called me in to dowse out what might be the problem," James said, "and I soon found out that it was the nature spirits. They weren't happy with her being there. We had to ask forgiveness for the intrusion into their space. They were okay then and after that she was able to settle in. She's now living there quite happily."

Troubles at boundaries

Nature sometimes brings destructive storms where trees are torn up and toppled. But they do recover and life goes on. Wanton destruction by humans, however, is another thing. I was painfully made aware of this problem at the time of writing, when a neighbour suddenly appeared with a large excavator in the next door field. Before we knew it the excavator was at our boundary, tearing away at the large limbs of the beautiful Oak tree, which is some 10m tall. This Oak leans over from our land across the little stream, which is an old townland boundary, to hang over the neighbours field. (Once considered sacred, the boundaries of Irish townlands once separated the territories of different clan groups.) We greatly admire this tree, the only Oak here, which happens to be the favoured haunt of our fairy queen and located on her energy pathway.

The horror of seeing and hearing those limbs being torn off so brutally was gut wrenching! Yet the friendly neighbour could not understand our feelings towards this tree, thinking he was doing a grand job of fixing the fence and making a drain there, by first clearing the branches that were in the way of the over-sized excavator. It was a delicate situation, resolved carefully without creating a bad feeling between us.

But we were left with the job of shoring off torn branches to prevent disease entering the tree. Meditating a few hours later and we could still feel shock waves emanating from the poor mangled Oak. A little ceremony where condolences were offered and rescue remedy sprinkled was held. But the question remained – how might this awful situation have been prevented? (Unfortunately trees are not properly protected by Irish law, when once, under the ancient Brehon laws, there were stiff penalties for tree damaging.)

Neighbourly relations are very important in maintaining the harmony of a place. When we move to a new home or buy a bare site, often neighbours will come over to greet us and see what we are up to. This could be a very good time to let them know about our values, how much we love the features of the land, especially those features that might lie on our boundaries in common. This could forewarn them to not upset us by interfering with any of those features and to discuss any such plans in advance.

Certainly boundaries can be points of friction in the landscape, so ideally we take stock of potential flash points before problems arise. It's interesting to discover that Irish territorial boundaries in ancient times were often places where shrines to the gods were located. I guess this allowed for inter-tribal gatherings in a sort of no-man's-land setting, helping to soothe any potential friction between tribes. (In Australia, Aboriginal clan boundaries often converge at shared sacred sites as well, I've noticed.)

Chapter 10: Co-operating with the land

> "Ask not what can a piece of land give us, but how can we cooperate with it?" Bill Mollison.

Loving the land

I once visited a commercial apple orchard for a dowsing survey, where the client was purely interested in the devic life I might detect there, especially in the hot house where her treasured orchids were located. Normally I am employed to dowse for geopathic or electro-stress in a place, such that causes discomfort or illness. On this job, however, it was a joy to visit the property and I was enthralled by the vibrant nature of the Apple trees that glistened with health and vitality. There were also very happy devic beings on the farm, including a lovely, gracious fairy in the hot house, which was no surprise, such was the good feeling there.

"What's your secret? It's such a fabulous orchard with a great feeling," I asked the owner, expecting to perhaps be told about some wonderful organic spray or biological growing regime.

"Well, we do love working in the orchards, our children do too. We enjoy being here so much, it's such a pleasure," she said enthusiastically.

Later I noticed that over the boundary fence, the next door Apple orchard was full of sickly looking trees and a 'bad vibe' was emanating from there. Asking about that property she explained: "That's the farm of my sister. My brother-in-law is a very negative person and he doesn't feel much for the trees."

Wow! I thought. A 'secret' so simple - the abundance and absence of love - was manifest here before my eyes. Such a wonderful example of the power of our feelings.

Westerners seem to have forgotten such basic facts of life, the joy of the birds and the bees! Meanwhile, the Maori people of New Zealand give us an example of excellent gardeners who have much sacred, loving lore in relation to the culture of the sweet potato (Kumara), in particular. They say that Rongo, the god of agriculture and peace, got together with Te Pani, the Earth Mother, to create the Peace Child, the sweet potato.

Consequently when tending the Kumara gardens one must traditionally always be in a positive state of mind, or the crop will be upset and grow poorly. Sadness or anger have no place in the Kumara garden and gardening is necessarily a joyful occupation. (More aspects of Maori gardening are covered in my book 'Divining Earth Spirit'.)

Deva gardeners

There are devas in our gardens who are gardeners themselves, tenderly loving the plants in the area under their care. They help to initiate flowering, seeding or whatever phase is imminent for 'their' plants. They respond well to humans who also have a love of plants and are often in awe of the human ability to create and care for plants on the physical level.

When we look admiringly at flowers and plants, says clairvoyant author Dora van Gelder, it is a "great source of gratification to the fairies... Love for flowers and a conscious invitation to the fairies to help is a way to come to know them and perhaps even to see them," wrote van Gelder, who observed their incessant activity in gardens, their constant engagement in the care of living things.

"It is a love of living things which is the great bridge between the two kingdoms," she added. Van Gelder observed that fairy gardeners put themselves into rapport with a plant, size up what it might require, then go to work flitting around the plant adjusting its energies with the energy flowing from their 'hands'. Born in 1904, she trained under the brilliant clairvoyant C W Leadbeater. In later life she noted that the land fairies are feeling greatly encroached upon, with their habitat being much reduced; and that the use of chemicals in gardens and farms is also very detrimental to the fairies' work.

These days many people practice 'co-creative gardening', based on the idea that devas and people can make a wonderful team effort together, if their assistance is consciously invoked. This idea has been evolving since miracles of plant growth began to manifest in a garden at Findhorn in Scotland in the 1960's, thanks to the assistance of the devas and despite a harsh environment. More recently the Perelandra garden in the USA has inspired a new generation of co-creative gardeners to follow suit.

One doesn't have to be specially gifted to emulate this approach. Particular formulas are not necessary. A sincere connection to the devic world is the start. Then, by dowsing, we can find out which devas can be most helpful to us and pose any number of questions to them by dowsing for yes/no answers. Or ask the willing devas to come forward to assist and be open to receiving their communications on a telepathic level. It's also a good idea to initially verbalise out loud what is intended to be done in the garden.

Sometimes I invite particular devas to join me at a certain time and place, making an appointment with them, to give them time to come forward. You can't just rush in! An initial short period of meditation, as well, is beneficial to getting me on a resonant 'wavelength' to connect with them. And daily meditation keeps me most sensitive and better connected to the subtle realms.

In recognizing the intelligence in all nature, one needs to warn any plants well ahead of any pruning or lopping that is to happen. Give them as long a warning as you can. Then warn them a day or so and then shortly before it happens, as well. You might tie a ribbon around a large limb, at the point where you intend to cut. Trees have been observed to withdraw their sap in readiness, as a result of doing this.

Avoid trimming plants in the bird nesting season (early spring to late summer). It's better done in late winter. Hedgerows need only to be trimmed every second year and on alternate sides each time, to minimize disturbance to both wildlife and fairy life. When pruning, leave some branches lying on the ground, for habitat and mulch, and also leave standing deadwood, which makes favourite perches for the birds.

Always check in with the garden devas to find out if they would be happy or not with any new types of sprays or regimes you want to try out. An example would be the story I told in my 'Stone Age Farming' book, where the spraying of a (European) Biodynamic preparation in an Australian bushland setting caused a short term depressive effect on the atmosphere and, presumably, the devic life there. By talking to the devas, visualising what you are intending to do in their garden, and asking for feedback, you might avoid such problems.

Dowsing in the garden

Some dowsers create lovely garden beds by dowsing where these are best located and perhaps linking them in with natural energy flows. In framing your dowsing search, you would need to designate which types of plants are planned to grow there. Another approach is to locate the best spot for a Tower of Power (which I have elaborated on in my book 'Stone Age Farming') and to create gardens close by, so that they can benefit from the most concentrated part of the beneficial energy field surrounding the Tower.

It's worthwhile dowsing for the exact spot to best locate individual plants, especially expensive or rare specimens. There are beneficial, neutral and non-beneficial locations for plants everywhere. It's a simple matter to tune into the plant, by dowsing, and to ask whether it's going to thrive or dive in the spot you have chosen. Otherwise ask if you can find the very best spot for it and search within the given area.

There is also a preferred orientation that a plant would like to grow (and it's nothing to do with orientation to the sun). So when transplanting, you need to turn the plant around through 360 degrees, until dowsing tells you to stop and thus is found the preferred position. I guess this helps a plant to connect into Earth's electro-magnetic field.

One can also dowse for ideal companion plants to group together, in beneficial relationship to each other. Taking the permaculture approach, one aims to have 'guilds' of plants that are happy to grow together, each having similar requirements of microclimate, cultivation, watering and feeding etc.

The culture of domesticated food plants goes back some ten thousand years and traditions often ritualize the ideal ways to plant, tend and reap crops. There may well be ideal methods of sowing and harvesting that are worth re-discovering. Certain ways of picking produce may prolong the life of the crop and keep the plant happy, so if you are in doubt you can always ask the plant directly, by dowsing, what feels best to it.

Problems with metals

"Metals interrupt energies," English dowser and author TC Lethbridge wisely stated. It's no wonder, then, that the mirrors of feng shui are so effective! The metal of the mirror definately reflects noxious energies away from a place. Unfortunately this can send it off to cause problems elsewhere, so I don't usually recommend that method.

In fact I advocate the avoidance of metals wherever possible in one's home and garden. Metals can conduct noxious energies and disturb beneficial energies. Traditionally the fairies would be most upset if metal (iron is the worst) is left on one of their pathways or special habitats. Metals disturb the fairies personal energies as well.

It could well be true, as some think, that the arrival of the Iron Age heralded many declining environmental situations. Austrian 'water wizard' Victor Schauberger investigated the problem of declining crop yields, due to reduced soil fertility and moisture, in the north of Bulgaria in the 1930s. This followed the change to tractor drawn steel ploughs. In the south of the country people were still using horse drawn wooden ploughs and enjoying bountiful yields. By experimentation he deduced that it was actually the steel that caused the problem. He went on to find that copper coated ploughs and other tools did not have this effect. Copper coated garden tools are nowadays being manufactured in a small way, but they are not cheap. I like to use a wooden digging stick, as do Aboriginal women food foragers. I find large wooden kitchen spoons useful in the garden too.

In Poland I was told that horse drawn ploughing of small fields is much more productive, economical and eco-friendly than using a tractor. Such old farming ways will no doubt make a comeback, as they are so suitable for family smallholdings. What's old will be new again!

Curvy gardens

One of the great tenets of feng shui is to incorporate curving features as much as possible into one's landscape design. This allows ch'i flow to slow down its pace, start to accumulate and provide energetic enhancement of a place. Circular shaped garden beds are good for this, with keyhole access paths leading into them. On a slope a curvy vesica pisces/mandorla (almond shape) fits well. Conversely, linear patterns convey ch'i flows much faster, just as a meandering river that has been straightened becomes more prone to destructive flooding.

Sun Ploughing

Certainly a wavy edge, such as a sine wave pattern or totally convoluted form, provides a greater deal of Edge Effect, an oft emphasized principle in permaculture gardening. The greater the Edge Effect, the more that can be grown, as plants have better access to light, air, moisture and our attentive eye.

Schauberger also suggested a similar approach in broad scale farming. He advocated not to plough in straight lines, rather to use 'sun ploughing' - making a sinuous line of furrows. These are ideally oriented north-south, to allow for maximum solar gain to plants.

One is also 'going with the flow' when fence lines and tree rows are not going up and down slopes, which exacerbates erosion, but follow the undulating contours of the land. Metal fences can be intrinsically problematic themselves. One needs to be careful that these are not cutting through ch'i paths, disturbing the feng shui. Several people have told me how good the land felt when all the old metal fences on a new property were removed. Ch'i flows are potentially restored this way, the land allowed to 'breathe' more easily, with a sigh of relief, no doubt!

Keeping Dragons happy

Dragon lines, the lung mei of Chinese feng shui, are energetic pathways occasionally found meandering through the landscape, similar to, but more powerful than, the fairy passes. Having emanated from an Earth chakra (an upward spiralling energy vortex) they provide pathways for the sinuous movements of dragon spirits and help to convey them through the air, land or water, both over and under the ground. These pathways exit the land's surface via a downward vortex.

River-like movements of dragons along their dragon lines are a source of vitalisation of the surrounding landscape, as they "leave behind them a trail of life-nourishing powers which can be absorbed by living beings", Marko Pogacnik notes.

A dragon on a Taiwanese Taoist temple.

Not long after moving onto my farm in Victoria, Australia, a pair of Earth dragons made themselves known to me in a series of lucid dreams. I had a dream of discovering, on a ledge on the side of a hill in the back paddock, a little doorway, a pair of doors actually, beside which lay a pair of bull's horns, suggestive of a votive offering. A strange wild creature was approaching and I hid.

Going to the spot in the paddock where the dream was set, I soon discovered, by dowsing, a powerful rising vortex located there, from out of which emerged a couple of dragon lines. This spot turned out to be the lair of a pair of Earth dragons, a male and a female one, each with their own yang and yin pathway. The paired dragon lines went on to meander down the hillside, cross over the centre of the pond and go up the next hill, to disappear into the ground in front of an Aboriginal women's sacred site there (a beautiful rock outcrop on the hilltop).

Initially the two dragons were a bit hostile to me and I was severely warned, in another early dream, against removing any of the natural rocks around their home. I didn't plan to move any, but realised later that the neighbour next door had been occasionally mining for rocks for some years. This explained the anxiety of the dragons and the ruling male hill deva. I assured them their home would be kept safe and intact.

Later it was time for a fence to be made across the hillside, to keep in my new llama flock. I had been rather neglectful of 'my' dragons and I was a bit worried about upsetting them. As I approached with a wheelbarrow full of metal fencing equipment I felt the dragons shudder in horror and they told me to STOP! I certainly did stop and apologised for not explaining my plans beforehand. They had nothing to fear, I did have a special plan, I told them (telepathically).

I went on to construct the fence using the metal sheep mesh, which was so abhorrent to them. But when it got close to the location of the two dragon lines I switched to plastic fencing, which I knew would not affect them detrimentally. I gave plenty of leeway, making a section of plastic mesh about 3m long for each dragon to pass through.

Nowadays, with the 'dragon gates' to pass through when out and about, the dragon duo are as happy as can be. I always try to keep all my devic friends happy and there is a wonderful feeling on the property and this has even been reported on by people who have never felt energies before.

Zone Five fairyland

As the furthest zone relative to the home, permaculture design aims to have a Zone Five wilderness area. This zone can act as a wildlife corridor, where minimal disturbance is made. Beneficial birds and bugs for your garden can proliferate here, as can the devas.

With the majority of devas in Australian landscapes being of the 'wild', undomesticated variety, who know nothing of gardening, Zone Five can be the best place for them. As the sacred temenos of Greek traditional gardens, the wilderness zone can be a perfect safe haven for these beings. One ideally seeks out any existing 'nature spirit temples', where devas congregate, and designates them as Zone Five areas, to protect the inherent sanctity there.

No deva stations to be found? You might then designate wherever you want a Zone Five to be and, if it proves suitable, hold a little ceremony there. This could involve planting a sacred tree, placing a little gift on an altar or installing a special stone or sculpture, and lovingly inviting some devas to come and live there. Create a space on your land and in your heart for the sacred. And leave the metal out!

From then on livestock will mostly be excluded, except for bees, or pigs searching for a free forest meal of mast (beech nuts and acorns) in season. A little firewood, seeds or wild foods might be collected there. A seat for your own peaceful contemplation or meditation might be stationed at the edge. Apart from that, your Zone Five is left to fulfill its own wild nature and there is something freeing within ourselves when we observe this zone. No need for our control, nature can do her own thing perfectly well, by being largely left alone. We nurture our own wild, raw nature at the same time.

Some permaculture designs aim for a small patch of forest wilderness to reach up close to the house, in order to enjoy the life and beauty of it. But keeping the large trees that might be found there far from the home is a better idea in wildfire prone regions, not to mention the thirsty tree roots and marauding forest wildlife that can devastate gardens that are too close. Keep large trees well clear of vegetable gardens too, unless you are growing things in containers.

A Zone Five Frog Pond is a much easier form of wilderness to have near the home. As a mini-wilderness area that's ideally adjacent to the home food growing areas, a Frog Pond is is also great for the larger scale garden or farm as well. Amphibious life can here proliferate, without ducks or fish to eat their eggs (some very small fish may be okay however). Keep pond edges wild, with long grass dangling into the water providing a ladder for developing little tadpoles to venture out of the water. If dense enough, the jungly edge will also exclude cats and other predators who like to eat frogs. In return, frogs do a great job in cleaning up snails and slugs from amongst your food plants.

Some wet springtimes down on my farm in Victoria the sound of frog chorus from a large dam in the back paddock can be near deafening in the house at times, but it's wonderful too! The drought has ended all that, but they are probably still there, hibernating in the mud, biding their time until good rains return. My favourite is the Pobblebonk and yes, that is the sound it makes.

Elsewhere in the world frogs are disappearing at an alarming rate, as they are the aquatic equivalent of the canary-in-the-coal-mine, reacting quickly to toxins in the environment. We do well when waterways and ponds are clean enough to support a healthy frog population.

Frog ponds can also be homes to water spirits, such as dragons. In May 2009 I met a large and amiable dragon in England's Malvern Hills, close to St. Ann's Well. The next day several clairvoyants I took to the spot were able to see its dragony features. Later I went to the well and asked for some dragon energy to come into the spring water that I was filling my water bottle with. No sooner asked and I was aware of a small serpent like being going into the bottle. I took this back to Ireland where it was poured into our Frog Pond, that had only been made a year before.

The young dragon is now growing nicely and soon after arrival I observed that Smooth Newts, rarely seen in Ireland, were living in the pond, as well as a multitude of frogs. Dragons often take on protective duties and my baby Malvern Dragon has been assigned the good care of the Frog Pond and its denizens as its joyful duty.

Whilst in Malvern I was told a lovely story about a woman in England, a keen gardener who was taken by surprise when a dragon made itself known to her and asked if it would be okay to leave its eggs in her garden! She happily agreed and was intrigued to watch, over time, the development of the young, growing dragons, who obviously felt safe there. She told my informant that after a few months the dragon babes took on beautiful rainbow colours and from this she deduced that the Rainbow Serpents of Australia must be of a similar ilk. (I have written much about dragons and serpent beings in my book 'Water Spirits of the World'.)

D-I-Y sacred sites

A sacred relationship that you develop with a special place can elevate the ch'i level there, allowing it to evolve to become a powerful point for peoples' communion with Earth, spirit and cosmos. The love you bring to such a place can be amplified manifold. Journeying there can take you into sublime altered states of being. At some sacred sites, studies have found, magnetic fields in the brain are greatly stirred up and this can facilitate visionary experiences. Many people also experience healing at special sites too. We need to fully value and treasure the ancient sites and protect them vigorously, while it's also good to create our own new sacred centres in the land.

Traditionally considered most sacred in the landscape was topography that was unusual or striking - the yang features, such as mountain tops, special geological features or big trees; or the hidden and mysterious - the yin caves, lakes and secret places. But sacred sites can also look fairly ordinary, to an outsider's eyes at least.

I remember hearing the story of an expedition in central Australia of mostly Aboriginal people who went off to track down an almost forgotten sacred site, somewhere far from civilisation. The white man who had passed on the story was also excited about the mission and he drove them ever onwards through wild country for days on end. Finally they told him to stop. They had found it, in the middle of a vast gibber (stone) plain that stretched from one horizon to the next. They got out and crowded joyfully around the single stone that was just a bit bigger than the rest, there in a sea of similar rocks. That was the sacred site, he was disappointed to report. Obviously its significance was in the invisible realms, only privy to the initiated.

To reclaim the sacred we can forge new traditions, reconnecting to Earth's Dreaming wherever we feel moved to, as long as the site itself is friendly. One approach is to connect with the devas of place by making special altars in their honour, as a visible sign of one's good intentions. Traditionally it was the 'Good People' themselves who dictated just where they would be happy to accept offerings. You might place special stones at such a location, which might be selected by dowsing, and these could also double as Earth acupuncture devices, as required.

Stones placed in the landscape provide a good means of anchoring our intentions. Crystalline structures in certain rocks, such as quartz and feldspar, have the ability to retain and convey energies and memory. You might think in terms of programming intentions into them. But always check first if the rock energies are going to be appropriate for your sacred space. Be aware that rocks found in the 'wild', as well as harbouring wildlife beneath them, will probably object to being moved. It's usually best to leave rocks where they belong. Always ask first before taking rocks and a quarry might well be the best source.

Beautiful stones large and small are great for creating labyrinths and stone circles, and these are best located by dowsing. Such stone arrangements can be energised with ritual walking meditation, thus bringing a focal point of stimulating or harmonising energy to the garden, and the wider region as well. Yang energy stones or yin stones can be selected as appropriate. (Energetic stone arrangements feature in my book 'The Magic of Menhirs and Circles of Stone.')

Special stones can also act as deva magnets, I've found. After I made two small stone circles, one of milky white river washed stones and the other of pink granite, soon afterwards Earth devas moved in and stationed themselves there. Surrounding plants began to grow much more vigorously around the circles and growth is lush all around. I've found devas stationed at most stone circles ever since.

Interactive use of stone arrangements can result in the attraction of other sorts of energies to them too. British dowsers have reported that underground water lines have been found to move in slowly from elsewhere, over the course of around three months. This could mean that water starts to course beneath your sleeping place, a potentially hazardous outcome. So it's probably best not to locate a powerful circle or labyrinth too close to the house, to avoid intense energy exposure of any kind.

A Power Tower is another type of energetic installation that enhances plant growth. Sometimes called a Paramagnetic Antenna, it acts as a wave-guide that collects solar magnetism, thus intensifying magnetic field strength in a spherical area around it. A Tower is often made from a tube of paramagnetic crushed basalt and it needs to be positioned over a downward vortex.

A Power Tower in South Australia

Towers can provide control points in the land, from where we disseminate our intentions. They can also give the devas a buzz! Often an air elemental (fairy) can be found attached to the top of such a Tower, I've discovered. Dowsing Irish Round Towers, very much larger versions that originally inspired the Power Towers, I have found enormous devas.

Towers may not be so good if located too close to the home, so check that the energy will be suitable for your own needs before making one.

For a more yin energy sacred site you might create a beautiful pond with yin rocks, such as white quartz or limestone, and planted with flowering aquatic plants. A pond plus cascade or Flow-Form with water that's solar pumped through it can be pretty enlivening too (and more yang).

Whatever you want do, always 'check-in' first with the spirits of place beforehand. Greet them with love. Visualise what you are intending to do and dowse to find out if they approve or not. If not, is there a better location? Or a better design or time? Are the people involved in the project suited? Etc.

The more you choose to connect into the devic kingdoms, the easier the communications get. On the other hand, if you become obsessed with the devas, that could be very ungrounding. People who are mentally unstable are also best to avoid deva contact and visiting devic haunts.

Chapter 11: Permaculture on a low budget

Don't you hate those coffee table books about gardening where everything looks lush, fabulous and easy? Those colourful plants, often in sub-tropical environments where the climate is benign, frost free and moist. If only you had that rich topsoil! Or perfect weather! And some money to spend on landscaping would be good too....

My personal experiences of setting up permaculture gardens on several properties were all bound by one very large constraint. I had the free time to develop them, but very little cash to spend in the process. Gradual development was the only possible pace.

Despite this, my first permaculture gardens grew to be highly diverse and productive. 'Gmelina Gardens' was a 5 acre plot at The Channon in northern New South Wales, a region where many people enjoy 'alternative lifestyles' in beautiful natural surroundings. I had a school-aged son and thus lived within a structured time routine. It was a lifestyle ideal for the keeping of animals as well. But it didn't allow for holidays, nor could I afford them. (These days, conversely, I travel a lot so can't have many animals and gardens can get quite neglected.) In the creation of Gmelina Gardens the Great Challenge was – how to create a diverse and productive food forest of useful and edible plants and animals with little money? I do love a challenge!

My first one was to improve the infertile sandy soil. The original owners told me that they had 'flogged' that bit of their farm in growing feed for the cows. A soil test showed several chemical contaminants too (the farmers swore they never used any!), but only in tiny amounts. What to do? That was the only good growing spot available, so I needed to get stuck into some soil improvement.

Manure would be an ideal fertiliser, especially if it could be deposited in-situ. A symbiotic combination of plants and animals was in order, harking back to the old style of mixed small farming, which can build and sustain the soil. (The 'Old Macdonalds' type of mixed farm mostly now only exists as a nursery rhyme, in the industrial Western world).

Getting livestock

Having developed a fascination with rare breeds of poultry, I brought a few lavender Aracauna fowl and brown Chinese geese to my new farmlet, and later acquired several other rare breeds. As feral foxes are always lurking somewhere in Australia, a secure fowl yard with high fences was in order. So I fenced off a square patch of the before-mentioned field, making a fox proof enclosure of about 12 sqm. This had a wire 'skirt' all around, going out horizontally for around 30cm, to deter the fox from digging underneath. A small night house was created from bits of scrap corrugated iron and timber. This was 'thatched' over with biscuits of straw laid down for insulation, as here, inland from Byron Bay, it can go from very hot in summer to very frosty in the bottom of the valley, on a cold winter or spring night.

A Chinese gosling being baby-sat
by Vikki, the Jack Russell Terrier.

The Chinese geese had a children's play house converted to be their night shed and we let them out each day to free range, eat the grass around the house and manure lawns in the process. A fairly placid breed, they would always alert us to any visitors' arrival with loud honkings.

In their own big yard the fowl scratched out grass, weeds and bugs in preparation for the planting of vegetables. For all their good 'tractoring' efforts they were also able to pay their way. I had paid 'top dollar' for heritage varieties of pure breeds and they were fabulous specimens! I got them breeding up and soon had more than enough eggs and the odd cockerel for meat. To cover costs and spread the rare breeds around, I sold and bartered excess eggs and sets of fertile eggs for hatching, plus chicks, other young poultry and point-of-lay trios for a reasonable renumeration. And the soil fertility in the fowl pen was becoming exponentially improved too!

Always on the lookout for waste materials for composting with the fowl manure, I discovered a small factory in nearby Lismore where brooms were made in the traditional manner, with locally grown broom millet. With a tall trailer load of millet mulch created each week, their waste problem became my good fortune and I was able to take a tall trailer load home as part of my weekly shopping trip.

The millet made excellent bedding ('deep litter') for the poultry night house and for mulching the rapidly de-nuded enclosure. There were also lots of seeds in it that the birds loved to eat, so scratching it over was a relished activity. Soon it was time to build another yard onto the side of the first, to move birds to fresh ground and start the process all over again.

I also began to diversify into other rare breeds of poultry. Buying day old chicks or fertile eggs, or trading the spare birds I had with other breeders, was a cheap enough way to diversify. I ended up with many breeds of fowl, ducks, geese, turkeys and guinea fowl. (Too many, in fact. They do say that the poultry 'fancy' is a disease!) Plus there were a couple of angora goats, always escaping to eat gardens, the pests! And a pair of pigs that we employed to root out the Madeira vine, a bad weed of the rainforest, the edible roots of which they loved to eat. (Is there anything that pigs don't love to eat?)

Soil improvement

I also made compost with whatever I could find, including the broom millet and sometimes, whenever the circus came to town, even elephant poo! The Indian elephant keeper ('Roger' by day and 'Rajah' by night) let us get quite close to the poor old beast.

The challenge to make great compost was often an adventure, involving a bit of good exercise and the result, when fed to the soil, was bigger and better vegetables. We also used our own manure for soil improvement, with special compost heaps to treat it. Our urine was collected separately and either went into the normal compost (as it is quite sterile) or was used for watering in a diluted solution (5:1) onto the root zones of plants as a top fertiliser.

The combination of manure and added organic matter (the broom millet), plus crushed basalt dust rock, all composted together was a potent mix and the vegetables planted with it did very well indeed. I was also a community teacher of composting techniques, so I had to be good!

I still had a bit of digging to do to remove weeds before planting out the original fowl run, but by then I had attracted a small group of helpers who wanted to learn about permaculture first hand. These volunteers would come each Wednesday for a morning of garden work, followed by a nice lunch.

Later they got to take bundles of veges home with them too. With that sort of help I was able to easily make a row of six large fowl yards and through these rotated the fowl from one to the next, planting vegetables after them, on a roughly fortnightly cycle. After a year or so, the soil fertility was fabulous!

Getting plants

So how to acquire the edible and useful perennial plants I needed for my permaculture food forests without much money to spend? A part-time course at the local TAFE (technical) college, provided free of charge, gave me new skills in plant propagation. It was so enjoyable that I went back and studied organic farming, bush foods and other great courses.

Soon I was building myself a large and inexpensive shade house to propagate plants in. I used long, free lengths of locally grown giant bamboo to make plant shelves with. (Unfortunately, rats took to nesting inside it and were hard to evict!)

I soon became a keen propagator, collecting seeds of useful, edible or beautiful native plants that I came across. I found it easy to grow large numbers of plants and it was always a thrill when seeds germinated and tiny shoots appeared. Old milk cartons with holes punched in the bottom or side made great free plant pots. Other pots were acquired at the tip, or by asking around for unwanted ones. Potting mix was created by mixing coarse sand with well made, fine compost.

Being in rainforest country I began to learn how to germinate the seeds of useful local forest trees. I had access to a grove of massive old White Beech trees (Gmelina leichardtii, a species valued for timber), which happened to be profusely seeding that year. They looked spectacular, covered with masses of big, bright blue fruits. The seeds were reputed to be difficult to propagate, but after nine months of various treatments and patient waiting they finally germinated. I then approached my favourite fruit tree nursery to see if they wanted any of my hundreds of surplus babies. Yes – they did! I was able to trade them for grafted fruit trees and thus fill the orchard up with diverse species and varieties.

Trading energy

The Irish tradition of gathering together with neighbours to help with the harvest is called the meitheal (pronounced mee-hall). After the traditional hand harvesting of the grain crops the tired and hungry gang would be treated with feasting, drinking, dancing and merry making. The advent of mechanisation brought an end to this.

Over in Holland community barn raising of timber framed buildings was also once a strong tradition, which transferred across to the United States. In England the Walter Segal Trust carries on this tradition, with owner builders coming together to raise each others' timber wall frames, designed by Segal. These types of community energy sharings have been the cement of much joyful social gluing, alleviating the hard work of farming and sheltermaking. (Conversely, the endless drudgery of solitary self-building in rural isolation is the cause of many a relationship break-up, I've observed in northern New South Wales.)

In my own experience of the frugal rural permaculture life, bartering and energy trading have been a wonderful way of life. There were plenty of like-minded people in my area to swop skills and labour with. I was also actively involved in the community LETS scheme. This Local

Energy Trading System meant I could get interesting part time employment and be paid in the local LETS currency. This I could spend on other people's produce or specialised skills for things I needed help with. One regular part-time LETS job I had was at a local permaculture plant nursery, from where I often took home plants that didn't look good enough to sell, which was a nice bonus.

I was also a 'WWOOF' host, taking in 'Willing Workers on Organic Farms', usually young travellers, who work for a few hours each day in exchange for food and longings.

The waste resource

In the Western world waste is totally rampant. But, looking on the bright side, someone's waste is often another person's resource. I always try to source needed items that are second hand and I avoid buying things that are new. This is doubly good as it saves on global resources plus personal finances. Australia is well endowed with shops selling pre-loved items. The thrill of serendipity at an Opportunity Shop (charity store), when some really fabulous clothes that fit you are found, is hard to beat!

I was once asked if it didn't bother me that my clothes were pre-worn by others. On the contrary! Not only are they well worn in and any toxic fabric treatments washed out, they usually have a nice vibration from the person who was kind enough to donate them to the charity. Anything unpleasant comes out in the wash anyway.

My other favourite store is the Tip Shop, where people can freely bring things for re-sale rather than incur the cost and environmental detriment of sending them to landfill. (Sad to say, Tip Shops do not exist in Ireland, my second home.)

Free stuff

In Australia, I've found, whatever it is you need, there is pretty much always something to fulfil the need that's lying around unwanted and not too far away. You need to be perceptive and creative with this. Developing that farm at The Channon, I became an expert in the Noble Art of Scrounging.

Gleaning in rural areas was once a way of life. This is where people gathered to clean up the fields after harvest, collecting any left over crop residue. Sometimes farmers dump a whole crop or won't even bother to harvest it, as prices might be too low to make it worthwhile. Some people these days also enjoy free food that they glean from rubbish skips and bins, thrown out from supermarkets.

In suburbia there are also potential free harvests from fruit trees hanging over fences, in parks or on nature strips. Excess fruit can always be bottled and preserved for later. Wild foods can usually be found growing all over the place as well, but normally these go unrecognised by the modern populace. Free food is, in fact, everywhere!

By growing or finding it locally we reduce our Food Miles in a big way - that's good medicine for the planet.

Chapter 12: Sensitive earthworks

Making an almighty mess of your precious land with earthworks is best done at the early stages of implementing a permaculture plan. While heavy machinery might be fast and efficient, it can cause great trauma in the nature spirit kingdoms (and you!). But it can also be done with sensitivity.

I have visited permaculture properties covered in ponds and swale systems (a sort of shallow terracing) that felt very disturbed energetically. From a geomantic perspective, a macho approach to permaculture can be just another form of rape of the Earth.

If we take care to check in with the spirits of place and ask for their advice, approval or forgiveness in advance, we can prevent their anxiety or trauma, which can remain as a residual tait in the atmosphere. Displaced devas can be advised on where it's safe to move to, or even gently 'herded' to a safe place. In my own experience, a sensitive, thoughtful approach can really make an energetic difference, I've found.

Preparation for earthworks

In 2004 I was living on my 15 acre farm, 'Mucklestone', in Victoria, south east Australia, having completed self-building the house over the previous couple of years. It was time to consider doing some major earthworks. There were two dams (ponds) that needed rehabilitation, having developed large cracks during the drought. They were now leaking badly and rarely held water. And there was a vehicle access track to be made up to the far end of the long, narrow property.

For four years I had been getting to know the powerful devic beings stationed around the property and had developed good relations with them. Geomantic power centres and energy lines are prolific here. There are dragon lines, vortices and, at a beautiful multi-coloured rock outcrop, an Aboriginal women's sacred site. This piece of sacred land is truly a landscape temple and a haven for nature spirits. But as plans for the eathworks crystallised and I communicated visions of my permaculture dream to the devas of the far back paddock, a decided feeling of un-ease and downright anxiety began to grow.

The old hill deva had no idea what a permaculture plan was, let alone a garden of any kind. The land had been a eucalyptus forest bordering onto a recent lava flow (around 7000 years ago) and it was once quite fertile as a result. Then from around the mid-nineteenth century it was stripped of trees and so began a downward slide of soil degradation from sheep farming, plus some gold prospecting. (This is a major goldfields region of Victoria.)

I just couldn't get the concept of permaculture landscaping across to this ancient wild deva and he remained fearful of the idea of big machines churning the place up. (I found out later that a neighbour had been occasionally mining the plateau next door for large rocks over the years. The devas would thus associate bulldozers with rapacious earth gouging.)

It was time to call in a clairvoyant friend for assistance. When 'Mara' (not her real name) visited and checked out the back paddock she commented on the feeling of anxiety and distress there. "Yes," I said, "and I'm anxious too that all the devas will be upset by the plan." I had been trying to reassure them that it would only be a brief disturbance and that native trees and orchards would be established afterwards. I made it clear I had no intention of interfering with any energetic or devic features that spanned the property. "But they still can't understand what you are planning," Mara relayed back.

I tried harder to visualise the planned events and sent out many advance 'sorrys' until eventually, with Mara's help, the devas finally understood the idea of gardens and improved ponds and, most importantly for them, that I would not be destroying their homes! They calmed down and the feeling of intense anxiety disappeared by the time we had finished.

As she left, Mara cast her eyes over the small dry dam in the bare front paddock and announced that there were no major devas in the vicinity to worry about upsetting. But she reminded me to give a general warning to any of the spirits of place just before the bulldozing began. Yes, of course I would!

A few days later another clairvoyant friend, Billy Arnold, observed a big aerial nature spirit, an air spirit perhaps, at the site of the front dam. Nobody had noticed it before. It was hovering over the dam site, reminding him of a big white dove and also of a special deva he had seen years before at English sacred sites that he had dubbed the 'Holy Spirit'. It seemed, to me, that this new deva had come to energetically prepare the site, in response to our plan.

Dam building

We had enlisted Mara's help to warn the worried devas just in time, because six days later the bulldozer turned up to start work on the front dam. A big lake with an island for wildlife was made from the remnants of an old dam. During the making of it Billy observed a beautiful thing. As Cam worked on the pond with his big machines Billy watched a huge energy field, shaped like a hand, that came up from below the ground and also one coming down from above. These 'hands' were rotating in parallel to the Earth's surface, in a kind of massaging motion. They seemed to him to be bringing soothing, healing energy to the site, perhaps calming any frightened nature spirits there.

All went pretty well with ponds and the new access track, in fact things went better than expected. But the winter/spring rains had not been good in that drought year. I didn't want to take any chances with the new look dams. As my next door neighbour said later – "I could have been looking at an empty hole for the next 12 months". I had to go off on a trip interstate and so 10 minutes before leaving I went over to one of my Power Towers with some rain water and Tibetan bowls for a rain making ceremony. I flicked water onto the Power Tower and again apologised for the earthworks and, please, could we have some more rain too? Ringing the bowls I started to feel waves of energy pulse through my body, just about tipping me over on.

Billy had been watching from nearby and he clairvoyantly observed the whole thing. "Just then" he told me afterwards, "the big deva came up from beneath the Earth and surrounded you and the Tower. What a wonderful blessing!!" Indeed, it had definitely felt like one!

The aftermath

Sixteen days later I returned from my trip. It had been raining most of the time since my departure. The new dam in the front paddock was brimming full and resplendent with its little island. "How's your luck!" the neighbour said.

The energy of the place was so good as well! It felt magnified from the blessing of plenty of water in the ponds. The next time Mara was visiting she took a clairvoyant look at the front pond, where previously she had seen nothing in the form of large devas. This time she did have one to report. It was a big white dove-like being hovering over the waters, just as Billy had seen before (I hadn't told her about that yet, though). She said it was beaming down energy from a point in the centre of its 'forehead'. I suppose it was charging up the rainwater with energy and information.

Now when people come to visit they report on the wonderful feeling they sense. Even people who have never felt energy before, are able to here. The sense of the sacred is palpable and it makes a perfect venue for geomantic dowsing workshops that I occasionally run on the farm. The front paddock presents an idyllic scene and is filled with so much more life than before, with wattle trees gracing the dam walls (they grew with record speed!) and birds flitting in and out of them, water birds on the pond and kangaroos and llamas sometimes grazing around it.

The 'feng shui' is greatly improved and the devas are very happy and secure. All thanks to taking a sensitive approach and giving lots of warning, so that the devic beings could be prepared to deal with the rapid changes in their own way.

Chapter 13: Pollution and transformation

Liquid waste

Just as one person's waste is another's resource, the pollution that covers our beautiful planet is also often just wasted nutrients ending up in the wrong place. Our bodily wastes, for one, make fantastic fertiliser, yet they are dumped into the seas and rivers, despoiling and poisoning Earth's sacred waters. Excessive livestock keeping, way out of proportion with planetary balance, has resulted in mountains of manure. Concentrated manure is a plant killer that pollutes and sours the soil. Highly mobile nitrogen is able to leach from it into water tables and waterways, upsetting biology and potentially causing toxic algal blooms.

Mixing manure and water is usually a really dumb idea, yet it can be done in a smart way and even produce multiple yields for us. I'm thinking in terms of aquaponics, a relatively new concept that can integrate a small livestock operation, such as raising fish, ducks, yabbies (crayfish) or geese, with the production of edible or useful aquatic plants (water chestnuts, watercress, etc) Plants grow lushly on the nutrient rich water sourced from the animal ponds and they cleanse it in the process. The livestock enjoy some of the green waste and fresh water. In this way, a watery environment is manifoldly more productive than a dry one.

A series of ponds are connected together such that, after being cycled through them, the water coming out of the last pond will be clean enough to be released into waterways, or pumped back into the beginning of the system.

A series of Flow Forms, such as in this picture, add an extra water cleansing component in an aquaponics system. The swirling, vortical movement of water flowing through a set of Flow Forms helps to rejuvenate, oxygenate and purify it. Dairy farms often use them to help cleanse effluent.

Energised water systems of many other types have also been successfully used on farms and gardens, with beneficial bio-effects. A simple method is to magnetise water from the hose as you are watering, by attaching a pair of magnets around it, north on one side and south pole on the other.

Some people turn organic waste into compost from which they make a 'compost tea'. This is an extract made by soaking the finished compost for a few days, then energising and oxygenating the liquid with a pump, or by hand stirring or sending it through Flow Forms. Another technique is to make multipurpose compost enzyme brew, from fruit and vegetable scraps that ferment in an organic brown sugar solution over a few months. The resulting strained liquid has many uses, from crop fertiliser to cleaning agent!

Urine in the garden

Toilet wastes are best kept separated so that solid waste is kept away from water and dry composted. I have been using various simple systems over the last 20 years with no major problems. For urine, it's easy to have a small bucket for urinating in and it's best to use it fresh. Diluted urine is a great plant fertiliser, while used neat it can be a weed killer!

Urine has the lion's share of nutrients, compared to faeces, and we produce a healthy output of nitrogen, phosphorus, potassium and calcium and other essential elements each day. This perfect fertiliser can be employed in the garden on a daily basis, for watering onto the root zone of plants in a 1:5 dilution, or 1:10 for delicate seedlings.

In winter, if plants are not growing, you can just put urine into the compost heap, but try to avoid saturating any compost worms. Urine makes a perfect compliment to sawdust, so in winter you might have a sawdust filled wee bucket that's emptied onto the normal compost heap (not the humanure one) every few days. Being fairly sterile, it's all perfectly healthy and safe, unless you are taking hormones or very unhealthy yourself, in which case composting the urine is the better way to go. It's best to avoid wetting leaves with urine. Running it through an aquaponics system together with grey water directly to the root zone of plants might well be the go. This is an area where not enough research has been done and we need to get out and experiment and just do it!

So why should we not just buy 'cheap' nitrogen fertilisers? Commercially, nitrogen fertiliser is manufactured with intensive petrochemical and electricity use. I wasn't surprised to discover that over 20% of the UK's greenhouse gas emissions come from food and farming, with the manufacture of nitrogen fertiliser a major component of this (Food and Lifestyle magazine, autumn 2009).

While more traditional sources of phosphorus are globally in decline, meanwhile, our precious resources are being flushed away by sewer systems and easily forgotten. We take responsibility for our nutrient footprints when we manage our wastes on-site and don't pollute the environment with them. Recognising the high fertiliser value of our waste and using it for household food production makes this doubly worthwhile.

Humanure

Composting organic wastes is a kind of alchemy, as the original components are biologically transformed into a new substance that is fabulous for plant fertilisation. The same goes for our faeces, or humanure, although we need to take a few extra precautions that pathogens are well composted before use.

Dry composting is the simplest method. Using a toilet bucket, the simplest method, one adds layers of high carbon material as a balance to all the nitrogen being deposited. High carbon sources include wood shavings, sawdust, soil or dry and chopped garden weeds, leaves or grass or straw etc. Contents of the bucket should be composted separately in a special heap that is allowed longer time to break down than normal compost.

When the bucket is full its contents are dumped onto this dedicated, enclosed compost heap, to which garden waste, old compost plus an occasional sprinkle of lime and volcanic rock dust can also be added between layers. The heap is ideally made to be over a cubic metre in size. When full it can be turned out onto the spot next to it, mixed around a bit in the process, including adding moisture if it's too dry, before being left to finish, covered over to keep rain off. All up, a year or two can be allotted before humanure is ready for garden use. Compost worms can also be added to speed things up. But don't put worms into hot compost, or they'll cook! However, when you make a compost heap one day at a time it generally stays cooler than if made all at once, so worms should thrive and produce terrific vermicastings for your garden.

The most economical to build council-approved composting toilet I know of is the 'Clivus Minimus', named after the Swedish version that inspired it, the Clivus Multrim. This do-it-yourself version was developed in The Channon, New South Wales, which is where I built my two. A feature is the sloping chamber that carries the humanure and additives down an incline, during which time it's feasted upon by worms. Water from a hand-washing basin is directed into the chamber and provides just enough moisture to keep things well lubricated and worms moist. By the time it all reaches the little door at the back it is ready-to-use compost, completely unrecognisable from what went in.

Devas and compost

Biological transformations occurring in composting processes are assisted by the elemental spirits of fire, says geomancer Marco Pogacnik, who wrote a nice little anecdote on the subject. A compost heap in someone's garden was moved suddenly and a little flock of homeless fire spirits were left behind, wondering what had happened! Pogacnik had to help them move over to the new heap.

In Victoria I have a water-based toilet that's not really ideal, but it does the job. It's basically a septic tank system, inside of which a platform houses a worm farm and all waste water flows through this and out into leach fields. There's a wild world of wriggling life down inside that septic tank.

One day Billy Arnold made a surprising clairvoyant observation of the 'stink pipe' coming out of the septic tank chamber. "There's a big deva appeared out there. It's stationed over the toilet system, working with all the energies down inside it," he said, with a chuckle.

Who would have thought to find one there! We called it the Dunny Deva, of course. It goes to show that 'waste' really is wonderful! And the unsurprising fact is that our own organic wastes contain sufficient fertility to boost the growth of much of our food plant needs. By using them carefully in the food garden we can forget about buying in commercial, unsustainable fertilisers and close the nutrient cycle gap.

Chapter 14: Dealing with pests and weeds

What is a weed or pest? It's merely something we don't want growing or living in our gardens or farmland for some reason. It may be because it's an exotic pest with no predators to curb its rampant growth, or it could be toxic to other plants, livestock or people. The modern approach is to divide everything into the good guys and the bad guys, whereas actually some garden weeds are useful herbs or even wild foods!

So we need to discover a little about the weeds that are currently the 'de-facto cover crop' of our garden soil. A cover crop protects the soil from erosion, so your weeds may not be so bad after all. Certain weeds give expression to soil conditions that need to be addressed and they can be a useful rough guide to soil pH, nutrient and mineral status, moisture levels and compaction.

So study the weed's appearance and ask – what is it saying about this land? Likewise we need to discover which pests might be expected to turn up in the garden. Check with local gardeners.

When it comes to preparing soil for growing food crops people usually feel daunted by nature's wild abundance. To remove a thick mat of weeds the ground would traditionally be double dug, tilled or ploughed. Lots of hard work! These days many farmers use no-till methods, but unfortunately this often involves poisoning weeds with chemicals, before sowing seeds into a toxic wasteland.

Using an organic approach requires more effort and ingenuity. Although a one-off use of chemicals for weed control when regenerating native vegetation can be sensible to save energy and time, completely different approaches are needed where we are growing healthy food.

Some people use steam or flame guns to kill vegetation and these are fast, efficient and non-toxic. But the good guys can get burnt too! Then there are all the natural, home-made sprays such as diluted vinegar or undiluted urine for zapping young weeds, pyrethrum leaves or neem extract for bugs etc. These all have disruptive effects on biology, which need to be weighed up before use. Consider whether any beneficial creatures might be badly affected. And what would the devas think?

Slow weeding

An easy weeding and soil preparation technique might be used to do the job slowly over a few weeks in summer. Before weeds go to seed an area being prepared for food growing can be mowed or scythed and a thick sheet-mulch placed on top. This involves spreading nitrogenous rich material, such as stable sweepings with manure, or grass clippings, over the area. You might also sprinkle mineral additives, such as lime and crushed basalt dust across it too. The thicker the mulch layer, the better. Then cover all this over with a sheet of black builders plastic and allow a build-up of heat to rot everything down and kill the vegetation growing there, while creating freshly composted material for new growth. (I have also successfully killed off pesty trees by covering the stumps with grass clippings and leaving them wrapped in sheet plastic for a few months.)

Never leave plastic permanently on the ground, however, as it turns the soil sour through lack of gas exchange with the atmosphere. Alternatively you can use cardboard or lots of newspaper instead of plastic. Spread it thickly over the weed patch and do sheet mulching on top of that - layering straw or hay, aged manure etc. This is left to rot down while plants are growing in the top layer. They can be planted into shovelfuls of good soil or compost that are dotted around, nested into it.

Once gardens are established you will no doubt need to remove the odd weed occasionally. Manual control is best. Always remove weeds before they set seed. Or seedy weeds and diseased plant material can be burnt or well composted with other organic materials. To do this, compost is ideally made in the one go, with a pile of at least one cubic metre in size, a good carbon to nitrogen ratio (around 20:1) and 60% moisture.

Having noted these various techniques, by taking a permaculture approach we can incorporate smart design strategies into the garden, such that pests and weeds will never be a major problem.

Below the radar

Professor Phil Callahan, a radio engineer, has enlightened our understanding of insect pest and plant dynamics immensely through his studies of insect antennae. Callahan discovered that the bugs' antennae are tuned to pick up certain vibrations, including the scent of ammonia given off by unhealthy plants. This allows them to make a bee-line to plants that will make easy 'prey' for them to eat.

So how to avoid the radar? Callahan found that healthy, vital plants don't give off these signals and are thus largely ignored by the hungry bugs. So an emphasis on providing perfect conditions for plants to grow vigorously means we design to have healthy plants with no attraction to the insects. For instance fungal conditions on plants can be avoided by having a high pH (alkalinity) in the soil, which is best achieved with the addition of crushed basalt rock. (Lime is used traditionally to sweeten sour soil, but it carries a high energy cost in the process of its manufacture. Crushed basalt is a waste product from gravel crushing.)

Other cultural strategies include the selection of local varieties of plants with proven survival ability and avoidance of commercial hybrid ones. Natural predators of bugs can be encouraged or even bought in, while a rotation of crops ensures there is no build up of pest eggs or seeds. A typical traditional rotation of crops would be to grow root crops, followed by potatoes, then legumes, brassicas and back to root crops, etc.

Less pests in polycultures

The permaculture way to deter insect pests is to design for as much biodiversity as possible, so that insects are confused or overwhelmed by the variety of plant vibrations. This is nature's way. Conversely - vast monocultures of sickly plants growing on impoverished, poisoned soils are an equivalent of waving a red flag at a bull!

Polycultures can incorporate companion planting and guilds of mutually beneficial plants together. However not all supposed good companion plants turn out to be very effective after all, as modern plant trials have shown. Marigolds, for example, don't really keep insect pests away, although the closely related weed Stinking Roger can do, but it isn't half as pretty as a marigold! So one might as well use dowsing to find out which plants would be ideal to grow together.

Another tactic is to grow sacrificial plants that are dedicated to the bugs for their eating alone. After all – if you don't have any bugs at all, you won't attract any bug eating birds. It is typically the plant on the end of a row that is offered to nature. Then you just need to convey the idea to the insect devas and let the bugs munch away. No need for the warfaring mentality! This is a good, non-violent way to keep everyone happy in your garden. Just create extra abundance and share it.

Biodynamic approach

Biodynamic agriculture was inspired by Rudolph Steiner, following an unfinished series of lectures that Steiner gave in Poland in the 1920s. BD produce is usually grown in healthy soil, but BD farms are often monocultures of plants that can sometimes be challenged by pests and weeds. The approach they use is non-toxic and can involve harnessing cosmic energies to provide discouragement on an energetic level. Nature is used to counteract itself, as a homoeopathic dose of the pest or weed is made and applied. They call these preparations 'peppers'.

To make a pepper, a handful of bugs are killed and burnt to ash in a wood fire at a time of a particular planetary conjunction, when a strong anti-fertility message is imparted to the ash. This can then be ground in a mortar for one hour, in order to be 'dynamized', says researcher Maria Thun. One part of this ash is then added to nine parts water and shaken for three minutes. The solution is diluted thus again and again until an eight times dilution is obtained. This 8x potency, Thun says, "has been found to exhibit an inhibiting effect on the reproductive capacity of the pest when it is applied as a fine mist for three evenings in succession." For large infestations she recommends to burn bugs on the actual site of infestation. For larger pests you just need some fur, skin or feathers to make a pepper with.

There are simpler ways too. For instance Danish BD grower Birthe Holt had a serious slug problem that she dealt with by releasing some predator snails she was able to buy. But they didn't make much of an inroad, so then she made an extract of slugs. "When the moon was in Cancer I put 60 snails into a plastic bucket," she wrote, "filled it with water and put a lid on it. The next time the moon was in Cancer I sprayed the strained solution, a stinky, slimy substance, out around the garden and onto all the areas where slugs like to live. I also made a new batch. I did this three times. The following year the population went drastically down. I did not even make a new brew," she said.

Using the principle of radionics, which is a sophisticated application of dowsing and remote energy balancing, pest peppers can also be 'broadcast' from the comfort of your home, as a dynamic thought package. Or the message can radiate out from a pepper placed inside the top of a Power Tower or Cosmic Pipe, charging the surrounding energy field with its anti-fertility message. Appropriate timing may well be significant when doing this, so it's probably a good idea to dowse exactly when to do it and for how long to leave it in place.

Perhaps we are actually enlisting devic assistance when practising radionics in the garden? I strongly suspect that often when we are working with garden 'energies', devas are the intermediaries, even if not consciously invoking their assistance. The little fairies I discover looking down on student groups from the branches of trees are usually laughing. They are smarter than we think! All the more reason, then, to choose a non-violent approach wherever possible in creating no-go areas for weeds and pests.

Connecting and negotiating with the local devas can be an important aspect of working sensitively with the land for anyone who wishes to take that path. In respectful consultation with all nature, we can evolve wholistic, co-creative permaculture designs for sustainable living.

Small nature spirit shrine in a Buddhist garden, Taiwan.

Chapter 15: My Irish summer with the fairies

It'd like to share some recent experiences of the fairy world over the summer of 2008. In this example you will see how working with the local devas that share our space can be very rewarding, paving the way for harmony and occasional magical delight!

Discovering the land's magic

When I first met my husband Peter Cowman in August 2006, I visited him in County Leitrim and was taken to see the little greenfield site where he was planning to build and live. He had already constructed a small cabin there, but otherwise it was just a neglected field of thick grass and rushes, a low-lying, boggy meadow with a wild feeling.

I soon dowsed the presence of a nature spirit who presided over the site. She was shy, but seemed quite open to us. Her haunt was in the 'Fairy Dell', around the young Oak tree that provided us with a mantle of thick shade on that warm sunny day. This medium sized 'fairy queen' was sitting on a horizontal branch above Peter. (I later discovered, by means of dowsing, that we could call her Jinka.)

I also detected a 'green ribbon' flowing by that Oak (that is, a small, serpentine Earth energy line) and this diagonally dissected the whole site. Green ribbons connect patches of vegetation together and provide travel routes to facilitate the fairies in their gardening duties. I had not had much experience of green ribbons and I suspect they are not so easily found in Australia, where vast tracts of land have been cleared bare for broad-scale farming. Here in Ireland I would imagine they are much more common, with farm layout and hedgerow boundary lines fairly stable over hundreds, in some parts even thousands, of years.

Peter had already dowsed the presence of this Earth energy flow before my visit and he wanted to know if it would be detrimental for living there in the future house. He had had problems in getting the building project started and this was still the case when I returned a year later in 2007. Peter then told me how he often felt a presence when working outdoors, especially near the roadside hedgerow and around the wilder, southern end of the site. As a result of my initial prompting he had tuned into this presence, going around introducing himself to all the resident devic life there. Things had felt much better after that, he said.

I discovered a second deva, a gentle water spirit residing around the south end of the site, and she was a joy to behold. She had been stationed around a particular spot that Peter had previously dug for a soil percolation test. At a short depth down the digger had hit a spring and the hole quickly filled up with water. A branch of an ancient bog Oak was also fished out of the hole. I asked the deva if it would be okay to dig out the spot again and create a well there, or even a sacred spring, in her honour. Naturally she was impressed by the idea and has stayed fairly glued to the area, patiently waiting for this to happen.

Peter and I were married in Australia in April 2008 and, after a honeymoon in Bali, we returned to Síog (pronounced she-ogue, the name we chose for the site, meaning 'little fairy') with the intention of starting the next phase of building. The trees were bare after a long, cold winter. But after a few days of warm sunny weather they were covered with new leaf and the place transformed, with a succession of wildflowers starting to bloom everywhere. Three weeks of warm sunny days followed with only the odd dull or slightly damp day intervening. Good building weather!

We got back into our routine of starting the day with some yoga and meditation. When I still my mind in meditation I can 'see', with my eyes closed, when I choose to tune in to it, something of what is going on in the spirit world. Before long in my meditations I started to make contact with the nature beings. One day Peter and I were both simultaneously made aware of the presence of a happy little house spirit, living up near the ceiling in the corner of the cabin. I started to put out offerings to it, in the form of a little dish of food scraps.

We also placed food offerings on the deck of the cabin for the other devic beings. One morning during meditation, just after I had filled a tiny bowl with fresh porridge for them, I became aware of the presence of a little fairy. I could see it standing right there at the bowl, absorbing the essence of the offered food.

We relaxed and enjoyed the exuberance of summer, with green vistas so soothing to the eyes after coming from drought stricken southern

Australia. But then it was time to get serious about building. The first step was earthworks, as we needed an elevated rock pad to be able build high enough above flood level. The digger was booked to come on Monday May 26th.

Fairy warning

On Thursday 22nd I was very surprised to see, in meditation, several shiny green ribbons that radiated out from me and fluttering away. Fairies were about! The little one I had seen partaking of the porridge on the deck, plus another, were flying around me, tugging on the ribbons. What ever were they doing? Were they trying to get me down to the fairy queen's haunt? They were pulling in that direction alright. They may well have wanted to convey something to me, but I was too pre-occupied with other things and shrugged it all off. I even said, most emphatically, to Peter afterwards – 'I will not be a slave to the fairies!"

By Saturday I still hadn't gone to the Fairy Dell to try to find out the problem and all day I had had a horrible migraine headache. But I managed to rouse myself up and wobble down there and noted the regrowth of brambles and weeds that were starting to get untidy there, the pile of old composted branches and grass ready for removal. That lovely spot really needed a make-over. Unable to understand fairy language very well, we both felt that the fairies just wanted us to clean the place up for their frolic.

Over the next few days I tried to get the message over to all the resident devas that there would soon be the chaos and trauma of earthworks, but that it would soon eventuate in improved garden areas, new ponds and happy homes for all. This was no doubt a worrying message for them to receive.

When the Monday of the earthworks dawned, after meditation I was alerted to the unusual presence on the deck of Jinka, who was standing at the fairy food station. She summoned me out there. Was she cranky! Furious about the earthworks, she gave me an energy wallop! (This might have been the like of the 'fairy stroke' of Irish folktales.) It wasn't debilitating though and I showered her with apologies for the chaos to come.

Preparation for earthworks

Michael, the digger man, was late and didn't arrive until after midday. It gave us more time for preparation and this included going out early and walking slowly across all the areas to be dug (scraped of topsoil, then covered with rock), with arms waving, in an attempt to herd all the little devas away to safer areas. Dowsing afterwards indicated that the areas designated for earthworks were now clear of the nature beings.

The day of upheaval was short. The digging was done carefully and it all felt fine energetically afterwards. There were two holes for ponds and some bare patches of soil to be dealt with, but these would soon be fixed. Expected feelings of trauma were not realised, although there was still a slight sense of unresolved anxiety. Meanwhile, I was excited about the landscaping work ahead.

Magic flower crop

A few days later I was ready to start broadcasting seed of Phacelia, an excellent cover crop with beautiful flowers, for greening the bare soil. During my meditation that morning I was called out by Jinka, who again wanted to hold audience with me on the deck. (Though small, at around 600mm/2 feet tall, she was regal in stature!) So when meditation finished, I went out to meet her. Happy enough, she had got over the disruption of earthworks and was now concerned about restoring plant cover on the bare patches of earth. She beckoned that she had something to give me. I went up closer and stretched both of my hands out and felt her direct contact with me, our auras interpenetrating. I saw something in her hand that looked like a little red purse. She poured from it what looked like translucent eggs or seeds into my hands. I thanked her very much for them, imagining that these were to assist me with my seeding work. At that she left and, not being about to go outside and sow them just then, I popped them into my aura at belly level as a temporary 'pocket' for them. There I could feel them and see what looked like little tadpoles wriggling around inside each of my 'magic seeds' impatiently.

Together Peter and I blessed the Phacelia seeds before sowing them and these were then mixed with the 'magic seeds' and spread around the bare soil areas. Lots of rain came over the rest of summer and we had a magnificent field of lavendar coloured flowers there, a total visual delight and the bees loved it! It all felt very special too. Finally, so much rain had fallen that in August a flash flood swept across the Síog meadow and the Phacelias were finished.

But in other parts of Síog wildflowers are always blooming in succession through the warmer months, a constantly changing palette of hues and textures to delight the eye. And the best thing of all is that Mother Nature plants them all perfectly, unaided except to be allowed Her own intrinsic wildness.

Crone deva

Following the earthworks I began to have clairvoyant glimpses of a powerful Earth deva of female form lurking in the overgrown hedgerow behind the Fairy Dell. I had ignored her, kept busy, but intended to make contact sometime. Deciding to start to build the weekend after the earthworks, it was a busy time for other pursuits.

On Saturday morning during meditation the crone presence was again noted and this time I acted upon the visit. Knowing it was time to properly explain the plan for our building project, I set up a folding chair beside the green ribbon that flowed across the middle of the building site. This serpentine energy path comes onto the site via a lone Alder tree and flows over to the Oak on the south western corner via a small group of young willow trees in the meadow, on the site of a future stage of the building plan.

I tuned into the intelligence of the fairy pathway and everything became clear and obvious! It dawned on me that I had I been somewhat asleep at the wheel, with the fairies trying to get my attention for a week or more! They even showed me green ribbons and I had ignored them. The burning question for them still had not been resolved. The fairy pathway had already been disturbed and they wanted to know was more in store and could we work this problem out, to get a good outcome?

Over in the background the big Earth deva had stationed herself in a field behind the Fairy Dell, seemingly intent on overseeing anything that might affect her territory. I next tuned in to her and acknowledged her presence. The image I saw of her was of an old hag who sat crouching with one knee raised up, much like some of the ferocious looking Sheela-na-Gig carvings that are dotted across the country, I thought afterwards. She was the regional land protector and perhaps her help to protect the environment had been sought by the fairies.

Sheela-na-Gig, Cavan Museum.

Feeling very lucky to meet this being, I asked this dark, wise crone goddess what her name was. Softly she intoned a BBBerrrrr.... I asked if she was Brigid, the maiden sovereignty goddess. No response. Boann, the river goddess? No. I asked again and I heard BBB RRRR AAAA.

When some noises broke my intense concentration, she suddenly took off, striding away to the south. I quickly thought to ask her a sensible question – "Where do you live? A vision of the old 'fairy fort' up the road came to mind. Peter and I had been meaning to explore the two local raths, on a nearby hill of private forested farm land.

Reading in my Sheela-na-Gig book and on-line about Cailleach Bheara, I found descriptions of this ancient Irish hag goddess, who conveys fertility and protection of the land, fighting wars if necessary. She is depicted in carvings as ugly or naked, often crouching, and is found living in 'fairy mounds' on hill tops. Bheara's attributes fairly matched my local hag, so I felt especially blessed to have met a powerful Wisdom Goddess.

One day I decided to have a dowsing expedition to find Bheara's seat. I distantly dowsed the fairy pathway after it passed by the Oak tree and followed it as it flowed both above and beneath the ground. Further along I traced its path directly across the roadway, then was able to follow it up the nearby hill, to where two Iron Age 'ringforts' were marked on the ordinance survey map. Tell-tale circular earthen walls of raths were nowhere visible, but possibly they had been levelled by farmers, or they may have been obscured by the dense tree cover.

Standing on the small boreen (back road) I went into meditative mode and tuned into Bheara. I soon sensed her presence beyond, down in the wild forest. It was nice to connect with her and this was the first of many visits. One time Bheara appeared to me there in the form of a huge white owl perched in a tree.

Re-aligning the fairy pass

Meanwhile, back to that morning on the fairy pass, it wasn't long before I had hatched out a good plan to appease everyone. I decided to create a little garden beside the hard pan of the house and into it would be transplanted the baby Willow trees that the green ribbon currently flowed past. (They were growing in the wrong spot in relation to the house.) A ceremony would be designed to help the green ribbon re-route itself around the hard pan in order to avoid passing through the middle of the building. This should keep plants and fairies happy, and Bheara would be pleased too, I'm sure!

We started the building project a few days later and the first job for the early morning was to prepare the new garden bed and dig around the willow trees that were about to be relocated. I watered them well and warned all of our plan in advance. Then I asked the green ribbon if it would kindly move when the willows were moved and to follow along with them to a new position.

And so we went ahead with the plan and replanted the trees as kindly as possible, in the same orientation as they had been before. We bedded them in nicely, with a bit of mulch around them, watering them in with a few drops of Rescue Remedy. Sure enough, the plan worked and I was able to dowse that the green ribbon had indeed moved to its new position. The atmosphere felt calm and untroubled.

Before actual building started we conducted a little ceremony on the building site, asking for blessings on it. We lit a candle in a jar and gave food offerings, of apricots, honey and nuts. It was lovely. I had invited Jinko to attend and sure enough she was there and I saw her with her hand in the honey! That evening just before the candle flame went out, after burning all day, we started to arrange the railway sleepers that were the foundations of the cabin, across which the green ribbon had previously flowed. It all went smoothly and harmoniously and we quickly had half of them in place.

I had made a deal with the fairies that I would honour the integrity of their fairy pass and not leave any metal on it. But bicycles and wheelbarrows were being left on it by helpers and I was again summoned to see Jinka, by her fairy helpers, who appeared to me as a pair of swallows flying around my head, during morning meditation. I went over to the Fairy Dell and promised that the offending party would

be firmly told the rules! There I found an old rusty shovel head that had been stuck up in the Oak tree and removed it. After this Jinka was happy again.

The next month I had another unusual deva sighting during morning meditation. I saw a figure that reminded me of Cerunnos, Lord of the Animals, from the Gundestrap Cauldron (left). This powerful, highly evolved masculine spirit of nature came flying in cross-legged, landing in the neighbours field across the stream. It seemed that he was checking us out from over there and he moved about as if on a magic carpet.

Building blessings

In August the building of the cabin frame had been going along very nicely, without a hiccup. Peter had all the foundations ready and so we had a little blessing ceremony and buried a couple of little stones in the middle, before the next stage of raising the timber framed walls. These ceremonies always felt so good to do!

The wall frames were made and neighbours invited to come and help raise them up into position. This only took a few minutes, after which a nice little outdoor tea party ensued. At last now, there were four wall frames up and the cabin frame stood tall.

It was a time for the next blessing ceremony, to celebrate the space enclosed. One fine evening we gathered up some instruments to make sound, a pair of clapsticks and a bell. While the previous ceremony had been focussing on Earth for the foundations, now the element of Air in the framed space was in need of a blessing. As usual, the ritual format we followed was informal and organically organised.

The intention to do that ceremony was sent out in advance and an invitation to any devas who cared to join in was given the day before. When we went over to begin, I was not surprised to find two little devas playing around up in the top of the frame. Playful little Earth spirits - perhaps the leipreachán (leprechaun) of Irish tradition? - they live beneath our Elder tree. One was perched on top of the north end gable, the other was hanging, monkey-like, at the other end.

We ritually walked around the space in a clockwise direction, blessing each corner with affirmations and resonant sounds. After finishing I dowsed that the little leipreacháns were now both stationed opposite each other, on the top point of each gable wall. And very happy we all were too!

Peter and I migrated south to Australia that winter and didn't return to Ireland until May 2009. To get back in the groove, we conducted a lovely ceremony to re-link ourselves with all the spirits of place and energies associated with the building site. It was another delightful ritual!

I had given out a general invite to the devas in the days before, as usual. On cue, at noon the sun came out from behind a cloud and I sensed that all the familiar nature spirits were attending. We started by meditating. Peter had decorated a little altar table beautifully with flowers, Buddhas, crystals and stones, and had hung flower bunches around the cabin frame too. He had scripted precisely his wishes for the building project and so he read these out and rang his bell. I added a few words of blessing, then we went around to each corner, plus the centre point, flicking spring water on each post, ringing the bell and calling for blessings.

During our initial meditation I had identified that Jinka the fairy queen was standing behind us and that an angelic being was hovering over the existing cabin. This being was different to how I had seen her before, for she now not only sported wing-like appendages, but a fish tail too! The mermaid is a popular goddess image of ancient Ireland, where water is never very far away. Goddess Aine sometimes manifests as a mermaid maiden, when she isn't in motherly or hag form.

Dark lord of the fields

But the most awesome visitor to our ceremony was the masculine Pan-like being I had met before. I hadn't seen him this close up. Huge, he was almost as tall as the cabin and took up much of the inside space of it. His big head was horned and he was positioned directly behind our altar as if to more fully enjoy the ceremony. In the corner behind him I found the little leipreacháns, a threesome this time. They were standing there looking up at that Pan in absolute awe. Even the angelic being from above the cabin had by now come in close to meet him, hovering in front of his head and seemingly intent on communication.

I was rather awestruck myself! The great deva had a regal poise, a stance I'd come to expect from that highly evolved being that the Greeks call Pan. Certainly Pan never was 'dead' and I have met him before in other parts of the world. On this day, this mighty being seemed also rather down-to-Earth. He was just happy to join in our ceremony and add his special energy. It certainly felt brilliant afterwards!

A couple of days after in my meditation I remembered our meeting and was musing whether this devic identity might be a local Crom Dubh, once the prime deity of the Irish pantheon. I immediately found myself on his wavelength and he started to communicate with me, giving me the sense that YES! he is indeed old Crom. I marvelled that I had been searching for Crom Duhb all this time, in books, journeys, fruitless searches for sites etc, and now, finally, he had come to me!

The aftermath of our ceremony was that it felt as if we had all 'gone up a notch', our projects really blossoming, the place just glowing with the buzz of summer and building. Gardens began to grow phenomenally! Feeling well and truly blessed, for the next fortnight or so I was cooking gourmet meals each and every night! And there was another bonus. Feeling inspired, the very next day I started to write this book.

Alanna and the cabbage at Síog
they call 'Big Max'.

Chapter 16: Restoring the woodlands

We want natural woodlands!

We owe so much to trees. Trees give us, so generously, a multitude of benefits from their wood, leaves, bark, flowers and roots. They are also protectors of the soil, they help to create rain and are essential to healthy water catchments. Trees give us oxygen to breathe, while purifying the atmosphere, with some, such as conifers, able to absorb air pollution. They give us beautiful environments and habitat for wildlife. In most human cultures trees have been central to, and the engine of, ancient economies, until the last ones were felled ...

There is nothing more anguished than the feeling of shock and annihilation when forests are clear-felled and the land left in a wounded and impoverished state. In Ireland forest clearance was extensive from thousands of years ago, but at a much slower pace back then, although the resulting effects are similar. Lands cleared in the Bronze Age, such as those preserved at the Ceidhe Fields in north County Mayo, enjoyed a flush of fertility for the growing of grain. But that only lasted a few hundred years.

Changing pollen records tell us that pasture land for grazing then predominated. In other parts there was a natural return to trees, or the climate got wetter. After that, vast bogs developed with blanketing spagnum moss, the main plant capable of growing on acidic soil with an impervious iron podsol. Thus the land's fertility was permanently lost. Evidence for Neolithic and Bronze Age farming in Ireland is often found buried several metres deep beneath such bogs, which went on to become sources of peat for heating and cooking, and these days, even for fuelling power stations, plus many are famed wildflower localities.

In another extreme case of degradation, The Burren, in north-west County Clare, is a stark landscape of mostly bare limestone bedrock, riven by fissures inside of which delicate, rare wildflowers flourish, ironically making The Burren world famous. People had long assumed that this soil free terrain was scraped bare by glaciers in the ice age 12,000 years ago. But after the ice age it was actually open woodland of pine and hazel trees, recent research has revealed. The forest was found to have been cleared around 2,500 years ago and subsequently farming and grazing, with attendant soil erosion, continued up until the 1300's, after which all trace of topsoil was largely washed away.

Like northern Europe, Ireland was originally totally forested. Most of the remaining natural Irish woodlands were lost between 1500 and 1700, as a result of colonisation. This left the land bare and the people more impoverished. There were even laws enacted in the seventeenth century which banned people from harvesting timber from trees, when once, under the ancient Brehon laws, everyone was entitled to access to trees, enough to build their homes and satisfy their simple needs. By 1900 only 1% of Ireland's vast forests remained.

Nowadays around 10% of Ireland is devoted to forestry, this being the lowest level in the EU, where the average is around 24% (while Germany is 30% forested). A total of just 2% (130,000ha) is native woodland, according to a recent National Forest Inventory, CRANN reports. But the plantations managed by the state, which amount to about 80% of total forestry, are mostly monocultures of non-native conifers with only about 4.2% of them being mixed species and not necessarily native ones, says the Woodland League.

When the predominantly Sitka Spruce stands are clearfelled there are enormous negative effects on biodiversity. The nutrient depleted and acidic soil is extremely vulnerable to erosion and landslips, while wildlife habitat and drainage patterns are destroyed. Total devastation.

The ugly cycle is repeated when more trees are afterwards planted, with liberal amounts of fertiliser sloshed around, much of which runs off to pollute watercourses that are not given the protection of vegetation on their banks. This typical style of Irish 'forest management', plain for all to see when you travel around the countryside, is minimal and gung ho, as they have managed to sidestep EU requirements for independent monitoring of watercourses and the like.

It's is a world away from Sustainable Forest Management, which says that 'Forest resources and forest lands should be sustainably managed to meet the social, economic, ecological, cultural and spiritual needs of present and future generations.' This is from the 'Forest Principles of Local Agenda 21, Principle 1 (b)', a 'Blueprint for Sustainable Development in the 21st Century', that was adopted as part of the Rio Convention of 1992. Ireland was a signatory to these principles, although perhaps it has slipped from their memory.

Andrew St. Ledger of the Woodland League informs us that "One of the issues that they may not want to have had investigated [by the EU] is that despite the state forest company Coillte, who monopolise Irish forestry, having had Forest Stewardship Council (FSC) certification for nine years - they have <u>no</u> forest standard in place". Coillte's poor example of forestry is echoed elsewhere across the world, but more usually in the so-called 'third world' countries.

What to do? A forest revolution is needed! St. Ledger told me that the EU has decided that forestry is integral to rural development and that the preferred approach towards sustainable forestry is to encourage processes of natural regeneration and species succession. And this can happen with an almost 'do nothing' approach. John Seymour, the English self-sufficiency pioneer, wrote about these processes happening on his own land back in 1982.

"I fenced off 5 acres of land on my farm in Pembrokeshire against farm animals fifteen yeas ago," he said. "...The ground soon got covered with Gorse and Bracken, the Gorse gradually winning from the Bracken, and then, after about five years, I noticed thousands of young Birch beginning to grow through. Among these there was a sprinkling of Alder, in the wetter parts, and Ash in the drier. In one or two places there were young Sessile Oaks. ...I shall be surprised, if I am still alive, if in 50 years time the area is not predominantly Ash and Oak – chiefly Oak – and that this will become the 'climax forest'," he wrote.

Natural woodlands are not the only rare or endangered ecosystems. We need to recreate and preserve other natural eco-tomes, such as wildflower meadows, as well. Let the native flowers bloom abundantly, inviting in wildlife, bringing helpful birds and bugs that can then patrol your food gardens. (Beware of cheap wildflower seed imports from distant regions or countries, stick to local sources!)

If you end up with your own diverse meadows and woodlands you might want to encourage others to follow suit by becoming a seed supplier yourself. Not to mention all those wonderful by-products that a sensitive approach to small-scale commercial mixed forestry might provide - such as timber, firewood and coppice rods, wild mushrooms, resin, herbs and honey.

But the backyard is not going to be big enough. In a sustainable future, community based local economies need to have community forests to supply many of their needs. Natural forestry will be the key to survival, St. Ledger concludes. When there is no more oil to burn and plastic to mould we will need to become wild woodsmen and women again!

Sacred trees

I'm glad that the spiritual value of woodlands got a mention in those Agenda 21 Forest Principles! Trees have long been globally regarded as sacred holders of wisdom and healing for mankind, as well as divine guardians of the land. The great intrinsic value once placed on trees was also a reflection of the important economic and cultural values they held. To remove or injure any tree under the ancient Irish Brehon laws carried a range of stiff penalties associated with the value of each species of tree. To cut down a sacred tree was absolutely taboo.

The ancient Irish royal centres were distinguished by grand specimens of sacred trees, treasured as living symbols of the clan and its chief's power. During the many episodes of tribal warfare these sacred trees were often targeted by rival tribes for extermination. They must have been quickly replaced, as there are records in the Irish Annals of sacred trees at particular locations being destroyed on subsequent occasions.

Groves of trees (the nemeton of the Celts) have been the primordial temples for nature worship since earliest times. Often the most important ceremonies and judicial proceedings were also conducted beneath stately sacred trees and groves. In Ireland sanctuary was granted by law to those sheltering beneath the leafy boughs of certain sacred trees. Few of these trees were able to survive the onslaught of war and religion because of all this.

Examples of pre-Christian veneration of trees in Europe survive, fragmentally at least, in various folktales, and in northern European folklore we find many common story threads of tree themes. In Ireland there was even an encoded system of writing - the Ogham alphabet - based on the lore of the sacred trees and plants, each letter being the first letter of a tree name. Europe has a treasure trove of tree traditions.

In Sweden, up until the 19th century, Lime, Ash or Elm were planted by country folk to act as guardian trees of the farmstead. The Ash Woman

(Askafroa) deva was honoured with offerings of milk or beer. Norse mythology says that man was made from Ash (Fraxinus excelsior) and woman from Elm (Ulmus procera and U. glabra), while Yggdrasil, the World Tree was first regarded as a Yew, then later as the World Ash. Interestingly, the favourite weapons of the stone age were originally Yew spears (a 150,000 year old specimen was found in the UK) and later these were superseded by Ash spears.

The protective spirit of Birch (Betula pendula and B. pubescens) was invoked when its wood was used for babies cradles and its twigs for brooms. With such besoms one would ritually sweep out from the home the old energies of the year to make way for the new year, at around the time of the winter solstice. After this the besom was hung from the roof apex or above doorways.

Rods of Birch were used in annual ritual perambulations of tribal boundaries, such as the 'Beating of the Bounds' in Britain. May Day fertility rites often took place in Birch groves until the medieval church put a stop to it. But the people then began to bring Birch trees into their villages and thus the Maypole and its associated festivities were spawned. In Siberia Birch is honoured as the very World Tree itself, a 'deity of the door' guarding the way to the spirit world in shamanic practises.

I was able to meet the Silver Birch Deva myself recently, when taking a homeopathic dose of the tree for healing purposes. Taking a high dilution of the tree's essence, I was delighted to 'see', with my inner vision, the deva manifest within me, as a slender female cloaked in a shiny white birch bark coat and mask. Meditating with the homeopathic pill under my tongue, I could sense her gentle power, beauty and refreshing qualities. She quickly went to work on me and I soon felt much better. There are various health giving properties in the leaves and other parts of sacred trees. But I'd never experienced the Birch Deva by merely taking Birch leaf tea.

The Rowan (Sorbus aucuparia) is another tree that has been highly venerated as a protector. Considered fortunate to have it growing near the home, twigs of Rowan were placed above doorways to guard against misfortune, while its berries were worn to keep women safe. 'Life Rods' of Rowan wood were once used to ceremonially beat life into people, animals and fruit trees each spring. A threshing tool made from Rowan was once used for preparing grain for sacred cake baking. Like many trees associated with abundant life, Rowan was also sometimes associated with death and after-life. Druids planted it at sacred sites and invoked spirits by burning its wood.

Aspen (Populus tremula) was originally regarded as an oracle, with messages divined from the sounds of its whispering leaves. Its close associations with Druidry caused many trees to be axed in Christian times, from whence it developed a reputation for being 'unlucky'.

Elm trees (Ulmus procera and U. glabra) were once esteemed as mediums between life and death, humans and devas. They were called Elven in England and Elfenholz (elfin wood) in Germany. Since the Dutch Elm disease has taken its toll of mature specimens in Europe, the best avenues of old Elms are now found in southern Australia, where they thrive.

Hawthorn (Crataegus monogyna and C. laevigata), has been long regarded as the sacred fairy tree of Britain and Ireland, as was Alder (Alnus glutinosa) to a lesser extent. Haw provided nutritious berries for Neolithic people and it has long graced the May Day festivities of spring.

Often called the May Tree, its white blossoms adorned garlands and wreaths and it was associated with White Goddesses and fertility. Roman people placed twigs of it above doorways for protection, while the Irish planted it close to their homes for the same reason. The first milk from a newly calved cow was, in some parts of Ireland, given as an offering and poured beneath a Hawthorn tree.

Gnarly old 'fairy thorns' are commonly seen in Irish fields and beside sacred springs and wells, and to this day some people still visit the latter to tie rags to these 'clootie' trees (as in the photo). It is considered unlucky to bring Hawthorn flowers indoors, perhaps the fairies resent this thieving from 'their' tree. There are many Hawthorns growing in southern Australia and I have fairies living beside my largest feral Haw.

Another sacred tree fondly associated with fertility and beneficent goddesses is the Apple (Malus species). This magical tree can link us to

St Kierans Tree, Co. Offaly, a hawthorn tree
still visited on annual pilgrimages.

the otherworlds of spirit, while an Apple gift symbolises love and abundance. An Apple tree famously features in the Biblical story of Adam and Eve eating of the forbidden fruit in the Garden of Eden. Such fiction is obviously an attempt to outlaw tree and goddess wisdom.

A delightful tradition from Apple growing areas of England, particularly in the south west, was to gather around the trees of the Apple orchard between mid-winter and new year for a session of 'wassailing' (pronounced 'woss-olling'). Cider was drunk and offered to trees, along with cakes, and songs sung to encourage fruitfulness in the following year, to toast and thank the sacred Apple trees for the bounty to come.

The Oak (Quercus robur and other species) has deservedly been regarded as the king of trees, providing so many benefits from its wood, tannin from its bark and also acorns that were important pig food. Huge sacred Oaks were places of sanctuary and ceremonial gatherings, and their memories live on in localities in Britain where we find 'Gospel Oaks', 'Honour Oaks', 'Royal Oaks' and 'Marriage Oaks'. Oak is also considered to be a doorway between the worlds. Well-known oracular centres in ancient Greece, such as Dodona, with thundering Zeus (and also Jupiter, his Roman equivalent) feature mighty Oak trees presiding over them. Those all-powerful gods may well have evolved from thousands of years of veneration of the Oak devas there, some think. The Oak tree is known to 'court the flash', so it's association with lightning gods is understandable. Oak is more likely to be struck by lightning than most other trees, as it loves to grow over underground water, which is attractive to lightning.

Energetic investigations of the Oak finds a high level of electrical currents running through the trunk, Hageneder informs us. The wood concentrates iron and is said to be paramagnetic, as opposed to the bulk of vegetation, which is diamagnetic, Professor Callahan has pointed out. Dowsing finds there is a stimulating, yang energy field around a healthy big Oak, making it a good place to charge up your own energies.

It's no wonder Oak has been considered a tree of positive power, for enhancing inner strength. Homeopathic doses of Oak can convey this strengthening attribute to people. I took some myself recently and found that this enabled me to 'see' the Oak deva. He was a wild Herculean man of a being, all hairy/barky bodied and curly haired, wearing just an animal skin around his loins, carrying a big oaken club and radiating lion-like strength, but with an aura of great kindness and benelovence. He was good medicine, too!

Hazel (Coryllus avellana) is a small tree associated with fertility and wisdom. A traditional source of pliable rods for water divining, it was said to dispense the sacred nuts of wisdom. Used also to make druidic Life Rods from, in Greek and Roman myth Hermes carries a Caduceus staff of a Hazel rod entwined by two snakes, as a symbol of wisdom and the healing arts.

Elder trees (Sambucus nigra) belong to the Great Goddess of northern Europe, Frau Holla of the German fairy tales. Elder was the guardian of the farmyard and the Swedes gave her offerings of milk, the Prussians - bread and beer, while the Scots put out milk and cakes. She was also seen as a guardian at the threshold to the realm of the devas, the underworld in particular. For the Danes the Elder Mother protected households from bad luck, illness or evil spells. She could also convey fairy sight, while fairies were said to delight in playing in her branches. Elder was always asked most reverently before taking any of her wood and she was never totally cut down. Without permission granted, any resulting furniture made from Elder would be expected to be haunted.

'Hats off to the Elder!' was an old Swiss and German saying, and the same was said of sacred Juniper trees (Juniperus communis). Talismans against bad spirits or the 'evil eye', Juniper twigs in Britain were hung above doorways on May Day. In Scotland Juniper was burnt on thresholds at the festival of Samhain, to repel the spirit world that looms large then. A protector of fertility, Juniper was also associated with death and the underworld.

Pine trees (Pinus species) have long been venerated too. Being evergreen, they were seen as holding everlasting power, while they also provided important sources of essential oils for cleansing, fuel and waterproofing pitch. Just walking through a conifer wood has a toning, healing effect on our lungs. The bright light emitted from burning Pine was considered to be another of its cleansing powers. Ritual torches made from Fir wood were borne by Scottish people at Halloween as they circumnavigated their fields on a sunwise course, giving blessings of fertility to the Earth for the crops of the following season. In Greek and Roman mythos the powerful Pine was sacred to, amongst others, Pan, the chief spirit of vegetation. And there is nothing Christian about the decorated Pine tree of Christmas time, symbolising the eternal spirit of nature, it's lights welcoming back the lengthening, brightening days following the winter solstice.

Larch (Larix deciduas), a deciduous member of the conifer family, is a denizen of high mountains areas. In alpine traditions Larch is the home of the 'Blessed Ones', graceful, elf-like beings who are kind to people and animals. In other alpine parts we find the 'Blessed Maidens', dressed in white or silver, if you ever get a glimpse, and often singing sweetly.

The Yew (Taxus baccata) is perhaps the most sacred of all the European trees. Capable of enormous lifespan, of over four thousand years, it represents eternity and great wisdom. Ireland was originally called the Land of the Yew People and goddess Danu and family were associated with Yew trees, their names reveal. Totally toxic, except for the red aril around the fruit, its wood was favoured for making spears and bows and today old specimens are generally only found in churchyards as a result. Yews are connected with the cult of the dead, the crone goddess of sovereignty and the death of the old year at the beginning of winter. Bronze Age burial mounds had Yews always planted to the north of them. Later, around 3500 to 3000BCE, they were planted on an east-west axis and, later again, Anglo-Saxons planted them on the south side of their sacred sites. Its wood was also made into wands and, in Nordic mythos, Yew was the original World Tree itself.

There was also a Yew Tree that lived in legend beneath the waters of Lough Gur, in Ireland's County Limerick. This was a home of Danu/Aine, the goddess sometimes seen by the locals as a mermaid on the shoreline. The tree was said to be guarded by an old crone who sat knitting, while it's terrestial equivalent, the 2m/8 feet high 'Stone of the Tree' still stands not far from the south-western shore. Only seen every seven years when the waters were said to disappear, this tribal axis mundi, the divine tree on the lough bottom and its associated legends, remind us of the primeval power of the tree in mythos and the importance of retaining Earth's green mantle.

Plant sacred groves

Natural forest regeneration can bring back the woodlands and it isn't rocket science! One just has to keep out stock and control weeds, and over time trees will appear and self seeding will multiply them with increasing biodiversity over time.

It's also a good challenge to plant your own Zone Five wilderness from scratch. To reproduce original native forests you will need to do some local research and obtain a diverse range of native seeds sourced from as nearby as possible. Then the plants will be of the local genotypes, perfectly suited to the growing conditions there. Local seed can be propagated at the right time of the year or sown direct on-site. Apart from a bit of thinning, if saplings are too overcrowded, or some initial weeding, there should not be too much work to do. Once seedlings are up thickly and shading the ground, weed growth becomes suppressed and minimised.

You could find out what local, native trees in your area have sacred associations too, to include them in your own woodland. Don't be content with using non-endemic trees, unless these are already existent (but please do remove plants that are considered bad weeds).

To give an example of why this is a soundly sensitive approach, if you live in central Australia the local sacred species might well be the River Red Gum (Eucalyptus teretecornis) or the Emu Bush (Eremophila longifolia). I have heard of a reafforestation project in central Australia where it was intended to plant Eucalypts from another region to stabilise a riverbank. But when the local Aboriginal people were consulted one woman was not happy with the plan. She remarked that this was not a good idea as it would "confuse the Dreaming" of the land. Very good point, I think!

If you are aiming to plant a sacred grove why not include a winding pathway that leads to a central ceremonial clearing? Here, when the trees are towering over your head, you might rest and be rejuvenated in the green, unseen by the rest of the world, enjoying the peace and quiet, watching the wildlife, treating yourself to exercise or meditation.

Nothing can surpass the majesty of such a divine green temple.

Alanna as a Fig Tree Spirit, Sydney Botanical Gardens, 1987.
Photo: Chris Farmer

Chapter 17: Living energies of the household

Imagine

A lush tumble of twining greenery and purple Clematis flowers frames the door of this house. It's hard to know where the vegetation stops and the building begins. We have arrived at an imaginary eco-home somewhere in Ireland. On this bright sunny day you brush past the burgeoning vegetation to enter the Mud Room that is attached to the north side of the main part of the house, beside the carport and workshop space.

The Mud Room feels cool and inviting as you take in its features. You note how a clever use of space accommodates laundry, storage and plant processing areas, with lots of built in storage space, places for boots and coats, armfuls of firewood and the like. It's a busy room that fulfils many functions and it acts as a buffer zone between the Living Space beyond and the outside world, so essential on a blustery, freezing winters night. It's an airy, light space with several open windows giving plenty of ventilation.

Above your head strips of netting are suspended from the ceiling, allowing bunches of herbs, seeds and other plant materials to dry out naturally. Later, when fully dried they can be stored away in the wall of cupboards ahead of you, that also provide extra insulation for the wall of the Living Space.

In the laundry corner there are no packets of washing powder. But you do see a packet of special plastic balls for washing that somehow affect the surface water tension to allow deep cleaning without any soap whatsoever. More economical than soap powders, they result in cleaner grey water too. Now that's eco-smart!

You slip off your boots then head for the main part of the house. Through the door you find yourself in the large open-plan Living Space that's bright and cheery, thanks to lots of natural light. On your right is the small kitchen, adjacent to the bathroom, for the convenience of centralised plumbing. It's a compact kitchen, with lots of built in cupboards. You notice that there is an extra tap at the sink. This is for the rainwater collected from the roof and here it's used for drinking, after

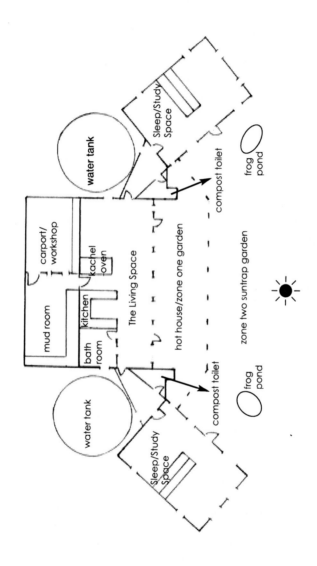

The 'Imagine' Eco-Home

some filtration. You have a few mouthfuls and it tastes very good. In the small bathroom the soft rainwater is also being used for washing.

Back in the Living Space you gaze ahead at another tangle of greenery, for outside there is a hothouse running along the length of the south-facing front of the building. Inside it is a fascinating collection of herbs, vegetables, shrubs, vines and small fruit trees, a wonderful Zone One mini-food-forest. From the dining table the views of this productive garden are delightful. Who would have thought that food gardens could be so colourful and attractive?

Solar passive design of this building has ensured that the high angle of the summer sun is kept out by its eaves, making the temperature just right indoors. In winter the warmth factor goes up several notches, as the house harnesses the energy of the more low-angled winter sun, while the captured heat is stored in its clay-straw walls that are painted with limewash, their whiteness also helping with the brightness factor.

Behind you there's a towering German masonry heater, called a kacheloven, a wonderful source of radiant heat from a minimum of firewood when in use. Thanks to the abundant scraps of wood from the local community forest there's always plenty to burn in this heater and with the high levels of insulation in the home it doesn't take much to heat it in winter. The kacheloven hasn't been needed for weeks, now that summer is here.

You sit down on the wooden floorboards of this timber-framed home and run your hand along them. Smooth, warm and welcoming. Tung oil rubbed into the wood has brought up the natural timber's beauty and there isn't the toxic plastic feel that a shiny polyurethane finish would give. Thanks to an unpolluted indoor atmosphere, you feel fresh and alert as you size things up. Time to check out the hothouse.

Going in inside you find the temperature more in the tropical range. You navigate a winding pathway that takes you to each of the raised box garden beds that are host to a range of lush fruit and vegetables. At the end of the pathway on each side of the hothouse you find a curious sloping chamber jutting out from the house. A quaint little wooden door at the front of the chamber has a sign on it that explains all. Behind this door, it informs you, is the end product from the compost toilet. Having slowly rolled down to that point it is now rich and ready compost that can go directly onto soil around the plants. The warmth in that south facing hothouse makes this a good location to assist the composting processes, especially over winter. You see another sign nearby that explains how grey water from the kitchen and bathroom plus urine is circulating around the root zone of the plants in their special 'wicking garden' beds, such that they rarely need to be manually watered.

Wandering back into and through the Living Space you notice just how comfortable you feel. The air smells rich from fragrant blossoms and natural citrus that were added to some of the oils for timber and furniture, the wood being all sourced from the local community forest. Local sheep provided wool for the thick insulation batts in the ceiling. There's a real feeling of being at ease in this beautiful home, which, although relatively small and simple, has a richness and aliveness that is palpable.

A door at each end of the Living Space leads to the two Sleep and Study Spaces. These are two separate little cabins that articulate onto the main building on an angle, to form the wings of a sun trap. You walk through the door on the left and into the connecting space between the two buildings. This is the location of the compost toilet. Going into the little toilet room you walk up a few steps, as the system needs to be elevated. You see that there is a facility for the separation of urine, which flows off to circulate with grey water around the hothouse garden beds for immediate use by plants.

Moving on to the next room you enter the Study, where a south-west facing window reveals views of the garden outside. You can see cute little dwarf fruit trees and a Frog Pond fringed with grassy edges, made when clay was being dug for use in the building. This must be the pond where the excess water from the garden grey water system is sent to, you guess.

A smaller window on the north-east wall gives views of the Zone Three permaculture orchard behind the home. This is a food forest with larger, ungrafted fruit trees and a berry, herb and perennial vegetable understorey. Beyond this, a small native woodland (Zones Four and Five) has been recreated around a little meandering stream that was once a totally degraded mess. The feng shui is looking good. On a low hilltop behind this a small wind charger is spinning around, silently making enough electricity for moderate power use. The owners built it themselves cheaply and they are happy to be off the grid. They even recharge their electric bicycles from the wind!

Navigating around a big set of bookshelves and clothes cupboards that form a moveable partition in the middle of the cabin, you get to the bedroom at the far end. Sitting down on the bed, you gauge that the sunset views from there might well be spectacular. Though not a big room it feels spacious, as the cabin is big enough to be formally divided into two rooms if desired.

This 6m by 4m cabin was the starter unit, the first stage of the home. The owner-builders were able to construct it fairly quickly and then live there comfortably enough while building the main Living Space. Later, when there was a need for a third cabin and enough money saved, the other wing was added. That made the south facing sun-trap garden complete, with cold northerly winds excluded and east and westerlies also, to some extent.

You step outside into the front yard and find yourself in the Zone Two orchard. Wandering amongst the compact dwarf fruit trees you are enchanted to discover a standing stone, a modern megalith. Carved onto it are wonderful sinuous swirling patterns and a shallow basin, full of water, on the top. A tiny bird that was bathing in the water flies off and, looking down into the smooth basin, you see the glint of golden coins in the bottom. You guess that this is an altar to nature.

Soft grass around flowerful fruit trees beckons and you find that it's a perfect place to lie in the dappled sunlight on this dreamy summer's day. You stretch out, breathe easy. Now that you have experienced the delight of an eco-home you may never want to leave!

House spirit

The home is not just our home. We share it with the other-dimensional world of spirit and there are many traditions surrounding various species of house spirits. In parts of Britain the front door, made of stout timber such as Oak, was once thought to be the home of a resident tree spirit that would act as a protector of the home and its occupants.

Green man carving, Poland.

Any structural timbers in the home were carefully positioned right way up by the builders of old, in the same orientation that they had been growing, so as not to offend the devas and harm the energy of the home. This was also the case for South East Asian societies, and no doubt elsewhere, with the root end of the timber used for a house post said to be 'planted' in the ground, reasserting its living qualities.

The Jorai of the southern Vietnamese highlands acquire a tree from the forest only with careful ritual to appease the tree spirit and prepare it for a new life in the home. Special invocations are chanted to appeal to these wild spirits to become domesticated and benelovent, Roxana Waterson informs us.

Houses in many societies were considered navels or axis mundis of the family, with navel posts in the centre of them providing the anchoring point for their power. A protective house spirit or Lord of the House, Ampo Banua hovers around this central post, according to the Buginese culture of Indonesian south Sulawesi.

In Ireland fairies were not usually known to intrude into the homes of humans, unless they happened to have been built on a 'fairy pass'. But there are exceptions. The Irish Banshee or White Woman deva is known to become attached to certain families, musical families in particular. They will even follow them in their migrations around the world and this has occurred with branches of the O'Grady family. When a family member is about to die the Banshee is heard wailing ominously near the house. Human keeners around Limerick's Lough Gur mourned in a similar fashion up until the early 20th century, Dames writes. The cry may also originate from a waterway or lake with which her name is connected; other times she is called the 'house fairy', Rev. O'Hanlon noted in 1870.

Another Irish nature spirit known to sometimes attach itself to certain families and frequent their homes is the Cluricaune. This rather mischievous sprite apparently likes to playfully vault and somersault about, and to also hang around in wine cellars (perhaps to avoid human contact). It's said to be protective of its home and family and to ward off danger or accident to them.

O'Hanlon wrote of another house fairy which can be very respectful of the head of the home and, becoming fondly attached to them, is happy to render service. It can also get rather grumpy and choleric if neglected, or its food offerings are forgotten or "not placed in the spot he has indicated by some peculiar token."

I discovered a house fairy in a most unexpected setting, in a tenth floor flat of a large concrete apartment block in Wroslaw, Poland. My friends had been performing Agnihotra fire ceremonies there during the previous year, as part of a scientific study of its effects. As soon as I walked into the flat I felt a certain 'specialness' in the atmosphere. Big, beautiful indoor plants there radiated health and vitality, with lots of care obviously bestowed on them. And I wasn't surprised at all when, by dowsing, I found a very contented fairy stationed on top of the largest plant. This discovery was a source of great delight for both the little deva and my friends.

A fascinating interview with a house spirit was related by the clairaudient home owner, Verena Stael von Holstein, in Germany in 2001. 'Miller', as he liked to be known, was the chief spirit of the old mill house. He started life as an Oak tree spirit in the 13th century whose tree was harvested for house timber sometime afterwards. As a house spirit his work then became focussed on checking the health of the millhouse's timber frames and co-ordinating the household duties of other devas. Miller, who came across as highly intelligent, was very fond of the mill owners and keen to explain about devic life. Asked about the lifespan of tree spirits, Miller said that they can remain active up until the wood completely rots away.

Marko Pogacnik notes that the tree deva is actually "on a different path of evolution" to the actual tree. It co-ordinates the work of the various species of devas who associate with the tree, from the small (like little flower fairies), to the large (such as Pan), and acting a bit like the CEO of a company. Tree devas can also leave their tree. Miller said that he liked to sometimes go off with his human friends for short outings. Tree spirits are capable of this if they have a piece of 'live wood', that's carried by a friend, as a temporary attachment point. They can also transfer themselves from a tree that has been felled, moving into a young tree nearby to take charge of its welfare. Or they can be assisted to do this, invited to travel on a piece of 'live wood' with you to a new home (tree) further afield, if needs be.

Building biology

Feng shui type traditions the world over say that the house is symbolic of the human form, with its inner and outer world, its window eyes and doors as mouths. This living 'being' is thus able to breathe and perceive, protect and nurture. But feng shui is closely tied to ancient Chinese culture and our modern homes are very different these days.

However the idea of the home as a living, breathing entity lives on in a more updated approach known as Building Biology. This is a holistic regime of appraising a building for its health and comfort aspects and any ecological or social impacts that its construction has caused.

One of the main tenets of Building Biology is to allow for breathability in a healthy building, which is designed to act as our 'third skin'. Just as our own skin facilitates gas exchange between our body and the outer atmosphere, our clothes, the second skin, need to also provide permeability to release gases. The home must provide this function as well, otherwise gases such as radon, a carcinogen for the lungs, can easily build up indoors, in areas where it is prevalent.

Principles of good Building Biology sometimes go against those currently being promoted for energy efficiency. A super-insulated home, for example, may be unable to breathe properly and this can result in 'Sick Building Syndrome'. A compact fluorescent light may save on power, but it emits a brainwave-disturbing flicker and has a depressingly dull light, with a mercury component that becomes toxic waste at the end of its life.

Another good example is the concrete slab floor. Billed as a must in solar passive house design, for its ability to act as a heat store in winter, the slab with its metal reinforcing mesh can also channel stray current from the electrical system and spread geopathic energies as well.

You can make sure the slab is well earthed or don't use the metal mesh and go for fibreglass reinforcement. But the high environmental cost of cement is hard to justify, especially when there are better alternative materials for heat storage. Concrete, also, cannot breathe, while it emits moisture for around 5 years after the building is finished.

A healthy eco-home, conversely, avoids concrete and metals, and is built of organic materials wherever possible. The electro-magnetic climate is kept as close to natural as possible too (so all those appliances close to the bed have to go!). Natural sources of lighting, such as skylight windows, and heating are also used. Designed to suit local climatic factors, with natural ventilation giving good air flow, the house site is always chosen with good geobiology in mind.

But despite being popular since the 1970's in German speaking regions, Scandinavia and other European countries, good Building Biology has not become standard practise. Building culture seems to be more about upholding the status quo and fuelling exponential growth of the economy, factors that caused the global economic recession that started in mid 2007.

Living Architecture

Animists everywhere have the view that a house has its own soul and that this is a protector of its inhabitants souls. Like the concept of manna or ch'i, the soul-stuff of a house is said to accumulate through the choice of materials and care of construction. Around the home sacred wood carvings, woven fabrics and the like can also convey a great accumulation of soul-stuff. Ceremonies conducted during stages of construction also add to its aliveness and richness, say the ancient traditions.

Irish architect Peter Cowman has acknowledged and updated such traditions with his own concept of Living Architecture. Fundamental to the good ch'i one aims for in a new home is the cultivation of self-awareness and the good feelings of its inhabitants, he believes. "The home can be designed to act as a nutrient in peoples' lives and aspirations," says Peter.

Good house design, for example, will actively address issues of territoriality, such that the occupants each get to have a space to fulfil their needs. When everyone has their own appropriate niche, when good building biology prevails and occupants are contented, then the home becomes a happy nurturing point, pivotal in their unfolding lives.

Peter finds the best way to achieve this with his clients is to teach them how to be their own architect, in a slow and thoughtful process that often uncovers stumbling blocks or hidden aspirations in their life. The house plan thus evolves as a reflection of who they are and who they want to be. "It is a synthesis of internal and external considerations", he says.
Too many people are building homes that they are tailoring to be saleable in the future to someone else, rather than addressing their own true needs, Peter has found. It's all because there is a false or inflated idea of the value of a home, based on money borrowed and sets of standards that may well be far removed from the precepts of sacred sustainability.

In Ireland itself there are vested notions of sustainability inherent in the culture of the standard modern concrete home, which appeal to the idea of permanence. It wasn't so long ago that the impoverished masses here mostly lived in crumbling mud hovels, so Concrete Culture today seems to me to be an over-reaction to the past. Concrete is really very user and environment unfriendly. But an influential 'concrete mafia' is quietly lurking and the Irish banks hesitate to lend money for all-timber homes, despite these providing far greater comfort and environmental sustainability.

Peter feels that all people are endowed with a 'sheltermaker gene' and that this just needs to be nudged into reawakening. He teaches people how to build their own simple timber cabin – the 'Econospace' - using an ingenious framing system inspired by Walter Segal's method and based on the 'Peter-Post'. It is an empowering experience for all and when the walls are pushed up into position by students there's a huge buzz in the air! (You can see this happening in one of Peter's You Tube films.)

"Give the mortgage the flick and build your own small, inexpensive home", Peter has been saying for 20 years. Mortgage originally means 'death pledge'. Now, in the midst of economic recession, with over 20% of Irish mortagees in negative equity and the prospect of enslavement to the bank for life for something of diminished monetary value, his warnings have come home to roost.

Freedom from the trap of the mortgage, which was the underpinning of the economic bubble, may seem an unattainable state, unless we choose to prepare for it. Freedom, contentment and joy can be our heritage yet again when we start to think 'outside of the box'.

Peter's Econospace with clay/straw walls at Síog in Ireland.

Chapter 18: Seeding an eco-future

Seed saving

I find it hard not to be a compulsive seed propagator. Those seeds so alluring, hankering to be allowed the chance for full expression, are like little magnets to me. I want to fill the world with sacred and productive trees and I have been doing so for many years now.

To find, share and reproduce plants that are beneficial or rare, and to be a food plant seed saver within one's community - thus we keep traditional agriculture alive and important genetic heritage circulating forever.

The hype that giant industrial seed banks buried in the Scandinavian permafrost will supposedly give us genetic security, as was smugly announced in recent media reports, is just not good enough. Seeds must be reproduced, as those of many plant species lose viability in storage. Such facilities no doubt allow industry to control and exploit our precious genetic seed heritage, but their technologies are bound to be self-terminating in the long run. Community seed saving and sharing networks are the way to go. Seed saver organisations around the world are fuelled by devoted volunteers who maintain seed libraries for members with a free exchange of seeds available, untouchable by commercial interests.

Jude and Michel Fanton of the Seed Savers Network have been indefatigable in their efforts over many years to raise awareness of seed saving issues in Australia and also the Pacific islands and Asian regions. In early 2009 they produced an excellent film on the subject, 'Our Seeds - Seeds Bilong Yumi', with brilliant footage of amazing Papua New Guinean farmers and their planting techniques, and local initiatives to maintain traditional garden culture. It also looks at all the related issues around heritage food plants, including the effects of modern globalised chemical agriculture and the 'new malnutrition' from junk food. But the colourful traditions of garden culture shine through the film (and a short clip is up on You Tube). Watching it reminds me just how poor the Western world's culture has become. And we think it is the others who are the poor ones!

In reclaiming the divinity of nature from the stranglehold of commercial interests we can all become sacred custodians of food plant seeds and learn again to value the agrarian culture with love and pride. Industrial style agriculture may well be the most widespread environmental evil in the world at this moment. But it doesn't have to be like that! Industrial farming is never going to be as productive as small scale, backyard, intensive, organic production. And it is far more likely to deliver lifeless food, social disintegration and bankruptcy. The small and slow approach is not only beautiful, but nutritious and satisfying too!

Cultivate good energy

These days in our ever-gloomy society it seems hard to do, but maintaining positive energy is needed more than ever in this world. It's not enough, for instance, to employ a feng shui consultant, have an energetic site make-over and then just sit back. Good energy needs constant attention, innovation and re-invigoration in order to be sustained.

We can cultivate positive energy within ourselves and we can attract and keep good energy circulating around our home, garden and wider community. There are many ways we might do this. Peaceful contemplation and a culture of non-violence can be practised in our lives, although in the garden we do need to get mean with the weeds sometimes! But we can do it in a loving way. Respect can be paid to bugs too, or, taking a permacultural, preventative approach, one can design around them. A respectful pact with the bug devas might also be made.

In the garden we can design to have a buzz in the air! An unbroken succession of plants flowering, with blossoms always available to nourish beneficial insects, especially the bees, is a great way to boost pollination of fruit and veges. Bees have long been held sacred in many cultures. Without them our crops would fail. Yet chemical agriculture is killing them off. A new breed of pesticides – neo-nicotinoid - has been implicated in the loss of one in three British bee colonies, and many elsewhere too. Nicotine has long been known to completely disorient and kill bees. Yet the power of the chemical companies means the British government is reluctant to ban their use, at the time of writing. Colony collapse doesn't happen in areas of organic production or native vegetation. So we can all help to save the bees!

Invite people to gather in your garden to get the buzz as well, by having some work swops or field days there. Sharing your vision can be uplifting and contagious. Planting the seeds of a sustainable future in peoples' minds is a valuable activity.

Having full moon gatherings around a Tower of Power is a great way to re-energise its energy field and is the best time of month to do this. By including a short ritual, with music or sounds and meditation at the Tower, your place can get really charged up! And as the seasons pass, the needs of the garden change, so you might also look at the set of intentions previously imparted into the field and make any amendments to them at those times too.

Celebration and thanks

I write this in Ireland at mid summer. Another St John's Eve has been celebrated with a get together with local friends around a bonfire on a hilltop, one of many glowing points seen dotted around the district that night. We made music and chatted and laughed as the sun's glow peeped up from the horizon and crept across it through the course of the night, such that it never really got dark. In pre-historic times, similar types of activities would have also occurred. Earlier traditions of bonfires at Bealtaine/May Day eve and the Summer Solstice celebration of the light were, in Christian times, transferred to the night of St John's Eve, June 23rd.

Now the crops are quickening in the fields as the farmers make haste to bring in the hay, before more of the typically abundant rain that makes this country so green and lush. Meanwhile, over in County Limerick, traditions hold that Aine, goddess of sunshine and Country, watches over the fields of corn at Lough Gur, from Her stone birthing chair, where She is stationed over the summer (corn being a collective term for cereal crops). At mid-summer Her work is done and the dark half of the year is ushered in at the solstice time.

On Knock Aine, Her nearby sacred fairy mountain, every year around 1st August people used to gather in the fields and, forming into ranks, would walk in procession sunwise around the hill and the moat at the summit, brandishing flaming cliars (torches of straw). They would then run amok amongst the fields and livestock waving their cliars to bring success to the crops and animals in the year to come. This high point of the solar year was said to also be Aine's wake, for She would now be departing from the land. Sometimes it was the fairy hosts themselves on that night, with Aine at their helm, who went about blessing the crops with their own flaming fairy torches. Fairydom and the welfare of the crops and animals being always strongly connected to the devas of the land in Irish tradition. Aine is a classic triple goddess and around Her hill and lake She is sometimes glimpsed, either as an old hag, or in Her maiden aspect as a young princess, or as a mother or mermaid.

At the end of summer the dark Lord of the Fields, corn god Crom Dubh presides over the festival of the first fruits, between late July and mid August. The most enthusiastically celebrated of the year's community festivals, it was continued into the mid-nineteenth century as the 'Festival of Crom Dubh and Aine' at one assembly site in County Louth. Such celebrations would have no doubt once included the honouring of this divine duo as the sacred stewards of the ripening crops.

Crom, or Black Stoop, was said to be stooped from carrying Eithne, the corn child, on His back, being the first weighty sheaf of corn given in tribute before He descended into the underworld each August 1st (- a change of calendars in the 17th century changed this date to August 12th). The seeds of next years corn would thus be mythically readied for cropping in the womb of the Earth Mother.

Traditions say it was corn god Crom who introduced wheat growing to Ireland and that both He and Aine taught its culture to the people. At autumn's start they were traditionally seen in their elder, wisdom aspects, with Aine ruling as Cailleach Bhearra, the winter hag goddess, then turning into stone on January 31st, and reborn again as maiden the next day for the spring festival of Imbolc, February 1st.

Each year at the great stone circle called Rannach Crom Dubh, near Lough Gur, Crom was said to enter into the circle down a stone lined passageway illuminated by the first light of the sun each August 1st. With his spear of life in hand, inside the circle he lovingly buried the corn seeds in a sacred furrow, dedicated to the crescent moon, the goddess. All these symbols being marked out in stone beneath the clay surface of the stone enclosure. Locally this day was called Black Stoop Sunday.

Later Christianity instituted alternative paradigms/propaganda, whereby Crom Dubh was evil, but generous! In Anglo-Saxon terms Lughnasa was known as Lammas – the blessing of the loaves made from the first corn. First fruits blessings became the domain of the church from 1843, but originally it was the main community celebration of the year. Several community pilgrimages to sacred wells and hilltops survive to this day in Ireland, where they are held during the Lughnasa period.

Going into the Grange circle, which dates from some 4,500 years ago, the Crom Dubh Stone looms the largest. When dowsing at this megalith I felt a distinct pull downwards and I got the impression that here is a portal into the underworld. (This site is featured in my film 'Thirst for Ireland'.) People leave monetary offerings beside this stone, so Crom obviously still has currency in Limerick. When my Melbourne based Irish friend, the poet and singer Mairead Sullivan, visited the Crom stone a few years ago a valuable insight was received there. She was profoundly affected by her experience.

When Mairead closed her eyes and placed her forehead against the Crom Dubh Stone, suddenly a vision unfolded whereby she "...saw a night-time scene of people in front of me," Mairead said "and on my right shoulder facing me, but looking up at the moonlight, was a face, I don't know whether it was a man or woman, but I could read their mind psychically. And this person was saying that he would passionately love to see the day when human beings would embrace their heritage of joy."

Getting together to celebrate the bounty of the land is no doubt a primeval yearning for sharing that lies deep within us. The remnants of some such celebratory practises, however, lie not too far from the surface. The first fruits festival still survives in its originally secular forms to this day, in parts of Ireland where animism has survived the longest.

On Crom and Aine's day, that was later called Lughnasa and many other names, people once feasted communally, or shared with their neighbours sacred cakes baked from the first corn of the harvest, at the end of the hungry month of July. The celebrations were often held on special hilltop locations, beside sacred springs or ancient monuments. Neolithic standing stones were often present.

Maire MacNeill made an exhaustive study of such Lughnasa sites and associations, although she missed the significance of the bullauns (a word derived from Latin, meaning basin). For often a bullaun stone has been noted at the ancient assembly sites, in the form of a large recumbent stone onto which a basin hole, or several, has been carved into the horizontal surface. These are plausibly explained as being basins for grinding corn. Surviving amazingly well from Neolithic times, a short imaginative leap explains the presence of several holes on the one stone. In my reckoning the multiple bullauns were probably integral to a Lughnasa assembly and would have been used for communal corn grinding, as a component of sacred harvest feasting.

You can even find these these enduring cultural icons re-located to now ruined churchyards, still intact after probably thousands of years of evolving ritual use (or perhaps the bullauns were there first?). Commandeered by the Church as baptismal fonts or for holding holy water in, people still leave coins in them today.

Traditions of some bullauns associate the water found in them with healing qualities. More mysteriously, round stones occasionally found inside the basins were presumably once used for corn grinding. They eventually became renowned as sites for working magic, with rituals of blessing and cursing still remembered (twisting the stones sunwise for blessing, or widdershins, for a curse), as in the bullaun pictured.

I find it extraordinary that many of these bullauns were able to survive within or closeby to churchyards, sometimes even sporting the name of a Christian saint, for added respectability. The bullaun in the photo had nine crone spirit guardians stationed around it, in a powerful circle of protection, so otherworldy security measures seem to have keep it well and safe. It is an extremely high energy site.

Fulacht fia have been another Irish mystery. These are the remains of Iron Age stone huts that housed roasting ovens and stone-lined pits. It's probable that large cuts of ox meat were placed in the pits and cooked by adding hot rocks to boil the water, although leather making has also been postulated. Piles of burnt stones, a hearth for heating them and a well for water are usually found in the fulacht fia. Clusters of them are often found and these also occur near megalithic ceremonial centres, such as Drombeg Stone Circle, near Skibbereen, County Cork. This fulacht fia was still in use up until the 5th century.

Fulacht fia can be explained as the communal cooking places for the great feast of Lughnasa and also Samhain, November 1st, when excess livestock were slaughtered and feasted upon, in preparation for the winter. Or perhaps the feast at the Drombeg Stone Circle was at mid-winter, as the axial stone there is aligned with the position of the mid-winter sunset.

Ireland's community feasts were often overseen by the local ruling families, with the chief gaining much social credit for the generosity he lavished. But these were really occasions for the ordinary people of the land to get together, to feast, dance, play tunes and sports, to socialise and make love after the long summer of waiting for the harvest.

In central southern Poland that most holy of icons, the painting of the Black Madonna, attracts pilgrims to the shrine in Jasna Gora, Czestochowa. Each year at Jasna Gora an annual harvest festal is the biggest pilgrimage and festival event in the country, attracting some 50,000 visitors, mainly farmers. They come to gain Mother Mary's blessing for their crops and relax after the harvest. (I wonder if the tradition of the Black Madonna does not have roots in a dark goddess of the underworld?)

During the Jasna Gora festival held in 2009 (September 12–13th) the International Coalition to Protect the Polish Countryside held a conference that attracted about 300 participants. The mostly farmer crowd eagerly listened to the 'Farmer's Bishop', an "imposing senior figure in the Polish church", who came out strongly against threats to the countryside, such as from genetically modified organisms, the 'free market' and the EU, the ICPP reported.

Traditions of joyful community connection are historically woven together with movements for change, as when we gather with others, ideas flow as strongly as the home brew. Not surprisingly, modern society wants to fragment us away from each other, with laws against unauthorised meetings and the promotion of the cult of individualism. Hopefully the local community will return to acting as a basic social unit. Community as the new family.

After all, as the Chinese saying puts us,
    'it takes a whole village to raise a child.'

In a culture of reverence for Mother Earth we can raise positive energy and give thanks for what we have been given so generously, both on a communal level and also individually. It is an act of humbleness and respect to do so.

There is no magic formula for how we do it. Particular dates aren't even that important. Spontaneousness is probably best! For it is the state of our minds that really counts.

Giving special thanks directly to the devas is an approach that is starting to regain its original popularity. It may also be creatively satisfying to make a lovely altar of natural objects onto which little offerings can be made and from where verbalisations of thanks might go out to the spirits of our fields and gardens. It's a nice way to keep in tune with nature, as we devote a short time each day of honouring the other-dimensional beings of our beautiful world.

At your places of thanking nature you might leave offerings – a flower or pretty leaf, a morsel of food that you like to eat or a stone basin or bowl of spring water. These might also double as a bird bath, multifunctionality being such a great virtue!

An informant of Lady Gregory suggested, for someone who had a large home and wanted to keep the Good People happy, that they might "set a little room for them with spring water in it always, and wine you might also leave, but no, not flowers, they wouldn't want so much as that, but just what would show your goodwill," she was told.

In the same vein the German house spirit Miller suggested that an offering could be given with the following words – "This is for you. I think it's nice and that's why I'm putting it here for you."

As for how long to leave food and drink offerings in place, Miller explained that it's good to leave them out for as long as possible, but only until they go off or become mouldy.

One might also be inspired to write the Good Folk a poem or sing them a song. They respond very well to music too. Before you know it, the devas will be reciprocating an exchange with you, sharing their insights and wisening you up.

For despite all the upheavals of history, the sacred dimensions of life still have a habit of prevailing in the end, I've found.

Indeed, the Chinese say that in the battle of yang versus yin, yin will always eventually win.

So I hope that you may yourself discover the yin wisdom of the world.

It's out there - and it's eagerly awaiting your touch.

Dowsing students at stone circles in northern Poland.

References

Chapter 1: Sacred perspectives
Moore, Alanna, 'Divining Earth Spirit', Python Press, Australia, 2004
Lovelock, James, 'Gaia – a new look at life on Earth' Oxford Uni. Press, 1979

Chapter 2: What is permaculture?
Diamond, Jared, 'Collapse', Viking Books, USA, 2005.
Mollison, Bill, 'Permaculture Designers Manual', Tagari, Australia, 1988

Chapter 3: Slow living
Solar Box Cookers International - *www.solarcooking.org*
www.slowfood.com

Chapter 4: Sustainability and Dreaming
Sveiby, Karl-Erik & Skuthorpe, Tex, 'Treading Lightly', Allen & Unwin, Australia 2006

Chapter 5: Earth awareness, self awareness
Moore, Alanna, 'Learning from Irish Famines', article at *www.permacultureireland.ie*
Moore, Alannna, 'Helping the Devas' , Geomantica Films at *www.youtube.com/watch?v=jApDqWhv0oY*
Moore, Alannna, 'Remineralising the Soil', Geomantica Films

Chapter 7: Geobiology and geomancy
Moore, Alanna, 'Divining Earth Spirit', Python Press, 2004
Pogacnik, Marko, 'Nature Spirits and Elemental Beings', Findhorn Press, UK, 1996

Chapter 8: Sensitive site analysis
Bradley, Joan, 'Bringing Back the Bush, Lansdowne Press, Sydney, 1988

Chapter 9: Harmonising your space
Moore, Alanna, 'Divining Earth Spirit', Python Press, 2004.
Phillips, Alasdair and Jean, 'Mobile Phones and Masts, the Health Risks', Powerwatch Publications, June 2004 edition

Chapter 10: Co-operating with the land
Moore, Alanna, 'Divining Earth Spirit', Python Press, 2004
Coats, Callum, 'Living Energies', Gateway Books, Ireland, 1996
Moore, Alanna, 'The Magic of Menhirs & Circles of Stone, Python Press, 2005
Logan, Patrick, 'The Holy Wells of Ireland', Colin Smythe, UK,1980
Van Gelder, Dora, 'The Real World of Fairies – a First Person Account', Quest

1977, 2nd edition 1999, USA
Moore, Alanna,'Water Spirits of the World', Python Press, 2008

Chapter 11: Permaculture on a low budget

Moore, Alanna, 'Backyard Poultry – Naturally,' Python Press, 1998.
Sharkey, Olive, Ways of Old – 'Traditional Life in Ireland', O'Brien Press, 2000, Ireland

Chapter 13: Pollution and transformation

Pogacnik, Marko, 'Nature Spirits and Elemental Beings',
Findhorn Press, UK, 1996

Chapter 14: Dealing with pests and weeds

Callaghan, Prof. Phil, 'Ancient Mysteries, Modern Visions', Acres USA, 1995
Bradley, Joan, 'Bringing Back the Bush, Lansdowne Press, Sydney, 1988
Moore, Alanna, 'Stone Age Farming', 2001, Australia, Python Press
Holt, Birthe, 'Working with Effective Biodynamics in Denmark', Biodynamic Growing (magazine), Dec. 2008. www.bdgrowing.com
Thun, Maria and Matthias, 'The Biodynamic Sowing and Planting Calendar 2008', Floris Books, UK

Chapter 16: Restoring the woodlands

Dick Ahlstrom, 'When The Burren was forest', Irish Times, July 30, 2009
Hageneder, Fred, 'The Spirit of Trees', Floris Books UK, 2000
Kindred, Glennie, 'The Sacred Tree', self published, UK, 2003
Dames, Michael, 'Mythic Ireland', Thames & Hudson, UK, 1992
Mac Coitir, Niall, 'Irish Trees - Myths, Legends and Folklore' the Collins Press, 2003, Ireland
Waddell, John, 'The Prehistoric Archeology of Ireland',
Galway University Press, Ireland, 1998
Kelly, Fergus, Early Irish Farming', Institute for Advanced studies, Dublin, Ireland, 1998
Callaghan, Prof. Phil, 'Ancient Mysteries, Modern Visions', Acres USA, 1995
Seymour, John, 'The Lore of the Land', Corgi Books, UK , 1982
'Pilot Project Proposal For Integrated Sustainable Forest Management in East Clare' and 'The Case of Ireland Funding Forests into the Future' by Andrew St. Ledger & Kevin Hurley of the Woodland League, Ireland, download from www.woodlandleague.org
Wilson, Andy and Lynch, Paul, 'Mayo Energy Audit 2009-2020', Sustainability Institute, Ireland, 2008 office@sustainability.ie
CRANN- Ireland's Tree Magazine, no 85, summer 2009. www.crann.ie

Chapter 17: Living energies of the household

Hageneder, Fred, 'The Spirit of Trees', Floris Books, 2000
Kindred, Glennie, 'the Sacred Tree' self published, 2003, UK
Weirauch, Wolfgang (ed) 'Nature Spirits and What They Have to Say – interviews with Verena Stael Holstein', Floris Books, 2005
O'Hanlon, Rev. John, 'Irish Folklore', Ireland, 1870, EP Publishing 1973
O'Farrell, Padraic, 'Superstitions of the Irish Country People', Mercier Press, Ireland, 1978
Pogacnik, Marko, 'Nature Spirits and Elemental Beings', Findhorn Press, UK, 1996
Dames, Michael, 'Mythic Ireland', Thames & Hudson, UK, 1992
Waterson, Roxana, 'The Living House – an anthology of architecture in South – East Asia', Oxford University Press, UK, 1990
Peter Cowman at *www.livingarchitecturecentre.com*

Chapter 18: Seeding an eco-future

Seed Savers Network - Their great film 'Our Seeds - Seeds Blong Yumi' (2008) - "celebrates the keepers of the seed, the farmers and gardeners who preserve and share the source of our diverse food heritage. Filmed across eleven countries with twenty tribal groups, the film shows that common threats to food quality and health have local solutions." The 57 minute film on DVD may be freely reproduced for non-commercial purposes. Write to P.O. Box 975 Byron Bay 2481, NSW, Australia. *www.seedsavers.net*
Gregory, Lady, 'Visions and Beliefs in the West of Ireland', Colin Smythe Gerrards Cross, UK, 1920
Moore, Alanna, 'Harvest Deities in Ireland: the Dark God Crom, the Sun Goddess and their Corn Maiden Child', 'Wiccan Rede,' Lammas edition, August 2008, also on-line at *www.geomantica.com* in Geomantica magazine no. 38.
Meehan, Cary, 'Sacred Ireland' Gothic Image, UK 2002
Dames, Michael, 'Mythic Ireland', Thames &Hudson, UK, 1992
MacNeill, Maire, 'The Festival of Lughnasa', University College, Dublin, Ireland, 1962 (reprinted 2008)
IPCC - International Coalition to Protect the Polish Countryside. *ww.icppc.pl*
www.cotcg.com/Crystal Grove Web/Sabbat Fact Sheets/Lammas1.htm

Backyard Poultry - Naturally

From housing to feeding, from selection to breeding, from pets to production and from the best lookers to the best layers, this book covers everything the backyard farmer needs to know about poultry husbandry - including preventative and curative herbal medicines and homeopathics, plus permaculture design for productive poultry pens.

The Reviews:

"A wonderful resource! Alanna Moore has provided poultry enthusiasts with all the information they need to raise healthy poultry without using harmful chemicals."
Megg Miller, Grass Roots magazine.

"The poultry health section is the best I've seen."
Eve Sinton, Permaculture International Journal.

"An interesting and worthwhile book that will no doubt have a lot of appeal for the amateur or part-time farmer."
Kerry Lonergan, Landline, ABC TV.

Stone Age Farming
Eco-agriculture for the 21st century

From Irish Round Towers to modern Towers of Power for enhancing plant growth. In this book ancient and modern ideas about the energies of rocks are explored for practical application in the garden.

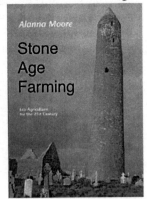

What reviewers have said:

"Simply fabulous!"
Maurice Finkel, Health and Healing.

"Quite fantastic."
Roberta Britt, Canadian Quester Journal.

"Clear, lucid and practical" Tom Graves
"A classic" Radionics Network.

"Will change your perception of the world"
Conscious Living magazine.

Divining Earth Spirit
An Exploration of Global
& Australasian Geomancy

"This book is a classic for anyone wanting to get involved with Earth healing. It contains information by the bucketload... The research that has gone into this book is incredible and no doubt will stir you into wanting to use it yourself"
Radionics Network Vol. 2 No.6

"Excellent reference book"
Don McLeod, Silver Wheel

"Love of the topic clearly shows, as Moore brings clarity and a sense of the necessity of personal involvement and engagement with the Earth. The great advantage of Moore's book is in its detailing all the salient aspects of Earth Spirit phenomena....all covered succinctly and with precision... the perfect introduction to the topic,"
Esoterica magazine, No. 4, 1995

"Highly recommended" Glastonbell Vol. 5 No 4

The Magic of Menhirs & Circles of Stone

Discover the world of standing stones, stone circles, medicine wheels and labyrinths. How to make them and utilise them for improved Earth harmony and personal benefits. Includes recent energetic investigations of these Earth mysteries by dowsers.

"Have you ever wanted a sacred site in your own back yard? This book will help you to achieve that dream," ... says reviewer Don McLeod in 'Silver Wheel'

The Wisdom of Water

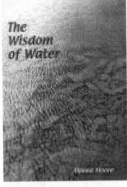

Water tends to vanish when human impacts are high. But we can reverse the trend and reconnect with the wisdom and healing powers of water.

In this 2007 book Alanna Moore delves into water's mysterious origins and manifestations; its energetic and spiritual aspects; global traditions; as well as water in Australian landscapes.

The potential of water divining, and 'new' water provides hope for a sustainable, water-secure future, she believes.

What has been said of this book:
"Very invigorating. Highly recommended"
Jilli Roberts, Pagan Times Dec 2007

"A great book!" Professor Stuart Hill

Water Spirits of the World
From nymphs to nixies, serpents to sirens

A follow-on from The Wisdom of Water, this book delves into even deeper esoteric aspects of water and its spiritual denizens.

What readers have said of this book:
"A comprehensive collection of information and a rich insight into the world of water spirits ... including some wonderful stories of encounters with water spirits ... well researched and informative"
Martha Heeren, Dowsers Society of NSW newlsetter, April 2009.

"A wonderful resource book"
Morgana, Wiccan Rede, Lammas 2009

This *"joyful travelogue of water spirits around the world has been a journey inspired by love"*
Anne Guest, Gatekeeper no. 26, UK

About the Author

Alanna Moore was a co-founder of the New South Wales Dowsing Society 1984. A professional dowser, she is internationally known for her writing and teaching of dowsing and geomancy. She lectures worldwide and also makes films. A permaculture farmer / teacher as well, her writings are archived at www.geomantica.com (as well as Australia's National Library), also at www.permacultureireland.ie

Dowsing Services

Do you sleep in a healthy place? Could there be a sacred site in your back paddock? Where to put a Power Tower to make your garden grow better; or to locate a stone circle site for meditation? And where do the local nature spirits reside? Find out with a geomantic survey by Alanna Moore. House and land surveys available by remote map dowsing to identify areas of noxious or beneficial energy.

One Day Workshops with Alanna Moore

Dowsing for Health – discover dowsing, our subtle anatomy, health effects of geobiology & electro-biology and how to avoid it, remote analysis and healing.

The Sacred Garden – How to harness subtle energies for enhanced plant growth and animal wellbeing. Geomantic permaculture design.

Divining Earth Harmony – Geomancy, building biology, map dowsing, Earth acupuncture & other Earth harmony techniques.

Deva Dowsing – Connecting with the energies of the Earth and its devic beings, landscape geomancy and Earth ritual.

Correspondence course
Diploma of Dowsing for Harmony

Since 1989 this course has allowed students to learn gradually, at their own pace in their own home, paying as they go (10 payments of $55).

Start whenever you like, $100 off for full payment in advance.

Comprehensive notes and dowsing exercises from Australia's most experienced dowsing teacher, Alanna Moore.

Geomantica Films
by Alanna Moore
Only available from Geomantica

The ART of DOWSING & GEOMANCY

140 minutes of dowsing and geomancy training sessions
with Alanna Moore, ideal for beginners. Price: $38 posted.

DOWSERS DOWNUNDER

102 min. of interviews and demonstrations with a diverse range
of amazing dowsers filmed around Australia. Price: $25 posted

Three educational documentary film series
by Alanna Moore:

EARTH CARE, EARTH REPAIR film series

Each approx. half hour/ 2 films per DVD. Price: $25 posted

Part 1: 'Dowsing, Greening & Crystal Farming'
Part 2: 'Eco-Gardeners Down-Under'

Part 3: 'Grassroots Solutions for Soil Salinity'
Part 4: 'Growing & Gauging Sustainability'

Part 5: 'Remineralising the Soil'
Part 6: 'Making Power Towers'

Part 7: 'Agnihotra / Homa Farming'
Part 8: 'Radionic Farming & Landcare'

GEOMANCY TODAY film series
Each film approximately half hour
2 films per DVD. Price: $25 posted

Part 1: 'Megalithomania'
Part 2: 'Divining Earth Harmony'

Part 3: 'Discovering the Devas'
Part 4: 'Helping the Devas'

Part 5: 'The Sacred World of Water'
(single film for $15 posted)

STATE of PILGRIMAGE film series
Each film approximately half hour
2 films per DVD. Price: $25 posted

Part 1: 'Glastonbell Dreaming'
Part 2: 'Pilgrimage to Central Australia'

Part 3: 'A Thirst for Ireland'
Part 4: 'Saving Tara'

Part 5: 'South Australian Sojourn'
Part 6: 'Bali - geomantic journeying in paradise'

See extracts of Geomantica Films on You Tube!

More films are in the pipeline.

Geomantica

PO Box 929 Castlemaine
3450 Vic Australia
eMail: info@geomantica.com

Free geomancy magazine and more at:
www.geomantica.com

Python Press Books

Available worldwide
For further information:
www.pythonpress.com
eMail: pythonpress@gmail.com

Living Architecture Centre

Peter Cowman BArch.
eMail: sheltermaker@gmail.com

Distance Learning Courses
Free online magazine at:
www.livingarchitecturecentre.com

Permaculture Ireland

Irish courses
Living Lightly magazine &
Articles by Alanna Moore
www.permacultureireland.ie

CPSIA information can be obtained at www.ICGtesting.com
Printed in the USA
BVOW03s2055051114

373918BV00007B/32/P